The Spiritual Meaning
of Rosslyn's Carvings

A Journey Round the Chapel

Written by
Jackie Queally

Illustrated by
Andrew Gilmour

Published by
Jackie Queally

You may wish to read the following book which is a complimentary guide to this book. Whilst this book deals with the exoteric and leads to the esoteric, the following book deals the reverse process, starting with the esoteric and leading to the exoteric. It also deals with the main letters of the ancient Hebrew alphabet that are co-creational codes still relevant today.

The Spiritual Purpose to Rosslyn:
The Key to an Ancient Matrix

Available at www.earthwise.me
and
www.celtictrails.co.uk/books-for-sale-2
or contact the author at
jackiequeally@gmail.com

For William Buehler
and all those committed to the process of Ascension

Copyright © 2014 by Jackie Queally

Illustrations © Andrew Gilmour

Second Edition 2014

All rights reserve, No part of this book may be reproduced in any manner without written permission except for quotations embodied in critical articles.
For additional information e-mail jackiequeally@gmail.com

Published by the author

ISBN

978-0-9930512-4-1

Contents

Acknowledgements 7
Foreword 9
The Tours 11
Introduction 13

Chapter One: 15
**Rosslyn Chapel and Roslin Glen
as an ongoing Creation process** 15

Chapter Two: 19
Numbers – Their Esoteric Function 19

Chapter Three: 23
The Central Axis and the Green Ley 23
    The Main Window 27
    The Central Axis 28

Chapter Four: 29
The Circular Route 29
    The Templa Mar and the Northeast 29
    The beehive 30
    The North Aisle 31
    The Temples 34
    The Sinclair Cross 43
    The Sinclair Cross and Christ Consciousness 46
    The North Door 50
    The West End 53
    The Main Door 59
    The South Aisle 65
    The South doorway 71

Chapter Five: 87
The Lady Chapel 87
- The Mari Pillar and the Templa Mar 88
- The Three Pillars of Wisdom 90
- The Journeyman's Pillar 91
- The Master Pillar 92
- The Apprentice Pillar 92
- The Four Altars along the East Wall 94

St Matthew's Altar 95
- Astronomical Alignments 96

St Mary's Altar 99
St Andrew's Altar 103
St Peter's Altar 104

Chapter Six: 109
The Nine Pinnacles above the Lady Chapel and Ceiling 109
- The Five Pinnacles 109
- The Four Pinnacles 110
- The Northeast Pyramid 111
- Inversion of Symbols 112
- The Ceiling 116

Appendices 119
Appendix A: Tours 119
Appendix B: Contact Details 119
Appendix C: Names of ENNEAD ANGELS according to Maia/Thoth 120
Appendix D: Two Studies in Astronomy 120

Acknowledgements

I would like to thank William Buehler for his metaphysical input on many aspects of the carvings. He has been a source of constant spiritual focus during the years I have known him. From time to time William Buehler checks the accuracy of his own research with gifted readers of the Akashic records – his main reference source here is Maia Christianne Nartoomid who has been channelling Thoth Hermes as her primary spiritual "benefactor" for nearly forty years. According to Maia/Thoth the Earth is under the mandate of Archangel Michael who is overseen by the highest archangel available to us, Metatron. I would also like to thank her for her indirect input (Contact details for both William and Maia are in appendices). Maia and her husband Simeon offer their deep service to the mystical community world-wide.

Andrew Gilmour is a retired architect and academic who very kindly volunteered to produce the drawings for the book, and his time and presence is very precious. His careful attitude to his work and the editing of the guide moreover was a most staying influence in the whole process. I thank him for his immense kindness and patience during the project.

My daughter Ruth has also been most kind in advising and helping with the layout without any prompting on my behalf. My thanks as always to her for her intelligent focus.

Rab Wilkie has cast his editorial eye over the text to fine tune it for final stage errors and did a splendid job, again freely offered. He feels like a gentle soul and enthusiast.

Ian Dinwiddie has yet again been there to support my work in the background, and as an active octogenarian he is a wonderful ally!

I would like to thank the ground staff of Rosslyn Chapel for their warm friendly attitude toward me over the years: some of them were most encouraging.

Finally, those clients who came from so many backgrounds and lent me their ears and also their own perspective—this has been a priceless gift. I know many of them have felt moved by their encounter, and I hope they continue to find places that inspire them to move toward the whole.

Foreword

This guide is an introductory mystical commentary that focuses on Rosslyn Chapel and to some extent its surroundings, as an area of exceptional spiritual activity and purpose. It takes you around the carvings so that they are understood to reflect a series of initiations into spiritual states of being, and also to reflect deep mysteries of creation. The guide is a natural extension to the content of my tours of Rosslyn Chapel that I have conducted regularly since 1999.

I have created a companion volume that is concerned with the details of highly evolved spiritual systems at play in Rosslyn Chapel, which have been detailed by my friend and colleague William Buehler. These spiritual systems manifest in a dynamic matrix of ley lines in the area as well as the overall design of Rosslyn Chapel.

The following information owes much to the brilliant work of William Buehler, an American who retired early from his Naval Commander career in order to dedicate the rest of his life to esoteric research. William shares and develops his research with others on the basis of a totally free global interchange of knowledge. The sheer volume of synchronicities and instant manifestations that have occurred in my life testify for me to the high level of accuracy of his knowledge and wisdom. He is widely regarded as an intuitive geomancer and mystic who writes prolifically on Rosslyn, other sites and sacred earth grid systems all of which relate to a wide spiritual system he calls the Reshel. The word "Reshel" is based on the Hebrew letter Resh meaning Chief Headstone (of God). William is also a creative student of ancient Hebrew letters, and from this study he has developed a body of knowledge that many perceive as ingenious.

In this and the companion guide I attempt to simplify some of the main ideas he has unearthed, at this critical time in our history. In my attempt to reveal these ideas with true simplicity I only ask that you will feel in your hearts whether this resonates with you as you read on. The Biblical references are based on his knowledge of the earliest form of Hebrew lettering, which he believes were designed as an energetic system of "light codes" for consciousness-raising and enlightenment. Later translations of the Bible are quite misleading with a view to interpreting these codes. From a metaphysical point of view the meaning changes and is lost quite dramatically when translating proto-Sinaitic letters into modern languages that are not consciously encoded with spiritual vibrations.

In addition to William Buehler's ideas this guide includes my own research and perceptions, and also valuable information freely given to me by friends, colleagues and specialists in various fields who I have met as clients. Some readers will find the guide may resonate with them within their own speciality if they have one. I would like to add that any comments re Clan Sinclair are my ideas and do not necessarily reflect those of anyone in the Clan Sinclair.

The aim of this guide is to aid the visitor to engage with the deep truths and mysteries of the chapel at their chosen level. Visitors to the chapel can enter and experience the place at any level, and return often to engage with the chapel at deeper levels. If they wish they may refer to the guide as a prompt to their own intuitive knowledge.

I believe that anyone visiting Rosslyn with awareness plays a valid part in accelerating the growth of planetary consciousness. It would be an understatement to say that this is crucial to our survival now.

The Tours

Since a young age I have felt that the earth is a sentient being (Gaia) and relates to and affects human consciousness in a subtle way. In 1999 I began to run tours to ancient sites that I discovered lay close to Edinburgh. Many of the sites were obscure and off the beaten track–places that bore certain charm and were associated often with old legends. Legends can testify to the sacred energies of the earth and sky, as the legends were born in a time when the culture was more sensitive to these things. From the start I included Rosslyn Chapel in the tours, and later realised that the site interconnects both historically and "energetically" (through the ley lines and geometric alignments) with most of the other sites.

Without my consciously knowing, the sites I chose also happened to relate closely to the Reshel pattern of ley lines in the area. Even after eight years or so of running the tours, sites I chose are revealing fresh evidence of their "telluric" (of the earth) energies of unusual intensity and quality, as new Reshel patterns in the locality emerge. The Reshel pattern is dynamically linked to consciousness or sentience, and as it shifts new patterns will emerge, particularly so in these times of immense change and growth. As I began to realise the significance of how the Reshel system of energies engages at a deep level with the mysteries of the cosmos, I met William Buehler and was invited to study with him. I am indebted to him for transforming a tourist enterprise into a very deep spiritual endeavour. In return many have been deeply touched in a myriad of ways by exposure to the sites.

Many of my clients feel that their path, whatever it happens to be, has been deepened from visiting Rosslyn and other sites with me. I would say that it is due to the energy of the sites interacting with Spirit through me, as the Reshel is a universal mystical language that threads its way through the sites once you begin to tune into them. I attempt to introduce people to at levels which suit their individual soul capacities. Often standing quietly for just a few minutes is all it takes for this to occur. It is not something that requires a great deal of planning, but it helps to be open and inwardly prepared for your consciousness to shift.

Finally, I hope you enjoy this guide book that has been on my mind for many years.

Jackie Queally
www.celtictrails.co.uk
www.earthwise.me

Introduction

In this guide I am addressing mysteries and not trying to simply duplicate historic formats found elsewhere. Where I do mention relevant historical notes it is because they are either interesting or supplement the mystical commentary in some way.

While in history many have followed the outer (exoteric) path of religion, there has always been an inner path for those few who have been called to follow another tradition – the timeless one steeped in mysteries and widely known as the esoteric path whereby one is concerned with knowing the divine in oneself rather than outside of oneself. Perhaps these paths are not mutually exclusive and they both can be embraced in one's life. This booklet is touches on the latter path, as we live in times when even those on the exoteric path may benefit from knowing that the esoteric path is alive still, and active in transforming our world for a better future. Everything in the world is made of varying energies born of thought forms or states of being that interconnect, and as we expand our consciousness we realise that our own state of being is dynamic and interactive with many other energies, bringing knowledge in their wake. Ultimately the Christ consciousness is a state of being that we can access only through divine grace.

It may be helpful to mention the universality of many of the symbols used in Rosslyn here.

When signs or symbols appear that seem to link with one another, if a higher consciousness or intent is speaking through these forms, they may not necessarily have been created by man in the same period in time. This guide concentrates on Metatronic energies that are high spiritual energies connected to the archangels Metatron and Michael. It is a metaphysical truth that higher reality works backwards and forwards in time. The energies of a sacred place are such that man – made markings or symbols are not necessarily generated in the same time period, as higher energies work outside of linear time. That is why we can see many symbols that appear identical in places wide apart and also set apart from one another in time. Mankind can link into these spiritual energies from wherever they are and ascribe them to a site, and in this way they depict the universal language of light simultaneously across the globe.

The initial inner efforts, when made without expectation or attachment to any desired effect can reap surprising rewards – in the same light Rosslyn was created in the hope that mankind would reach enlightenment and the world as an entity would find peace. So be it, and may it be so. The journey is now, not tomorrow.

Chapter One:

Rosslyn Chapel and Roslin Glen as an ongoing Creation process

When one is absolutely still, the greatest of truths can arrive in one's mind. The only way of accessing the mindset of those who designed Rosslyn is to enter that universal abyss and to listen to the higher universal truth that resides in the Silence (known in Hebrew as the Selah.). It is referred to in the Jewish Scriptures in the following passage

"The earth and all the inhabitants thereof are dissolved: I bear up the pillars of it. Selah."

Psalm 75:3

When we live from moment to moment in this manner of stillness, a higher world is revealed in which we can view the principles of Creation. It is in the Here and Now that we become elements of Creation itself, as we merge with those forces that lie behind the manifestations in our linear world.

The carvings in Rosslyn stem from many traditions including the Jewish Scriptures, and are much more than a cacophony of symbols to titilate the senses: they are placed according to a higher harmony that cannot be fathomed by intellect alone. The stones are outward expressions of spiritual energies discernible to those who seek in the silence.

One reason why each carving will generate many interpretations and layers of meaning is because we come to it from our own perspective, which is ever changing while we live and learn. The knowledge that is contained at Rosslyn is beyond what we can discern if we view life from our own linear perspective – it is through the inner eye that one can behold a state outside linear time in which everything co-exists. Such knowledge surfaces in different places and in different times but is essentially the same energy manifesting. William Buehler calls this state the Metatronic full light spectrum from which our world fell in the past and to which it is rapidly returning. In order to make the return journey the planet has to create new systems etherically to deal with the incoming new higher energies – in other words the planet is in a state of flux not just in our physical realm but on the various etheric levels that exist also. The high Archangel Metatron guides the universe to its real spiritual home, with the Archangel Michael chief guardian for our planet in this time continuum.

Not only is the placement of the carvings in the chapel describing a sequence of knowledge and self awakening that precedes any planetary shift in awakening, but the wider landscape and cosmic influences are brought into the chapel via its complex leys and further boost the spiritual qualities of the chapel. Leys, or ley lines, are alignments of energy flows usually associated with the land, which can be perceived by sensitive people. A simple way of discovering the ley lines is by practising the ancient art of dowsing, using divining rods of various kinds. When an area holds strong ley-lines it often is described as an active area. Roslin Glen, a small river valley that lies immediately below the chapel, is infused with high elementals (spirits of the earth) that are hard to access. It is even more spiritually energetic an area than the chapel, for the veil is thin in the glen, and many visitors can discern this as a place of true magic.

The chapel maximises its location by utilizing the leys to its full advantage in order to boost its own frequencies and become a chapel of intense spiritual light. The leys are not only set within the wider hinterland; they also are contained within subsystems of the chapel layout, demarcated by the layout of the pillars and steeples. These subsystems of leys further amplify the energetic content of the chapel and will be explored in the companion guide entitled "The Rosslyn Matrix".

When matter is in the process of creation there is a two way etheric flow of energy or information. For example, this two way poles for the energy that flows in both directions. Even though poles for the energy that flows in both directions. Even though earth energy may be felt as flowing one way it is on a higher reality plane flowing both ways constantly. The poles are detected as female and male at either extreme but in the higher reality that Rosslyn is concerned with the polarities continually switch to accommodate shifts in the energies. The layout of pillars and carvings in the chapel reflect this dynamic also... Rosslyn is cleverly crafted so that it is connected to both the outer and inner paths to Truth, in much the same way as there is a two way flow of knowledge between matter and spirit. The two directions or streams of knowledge are known in Christian esoteric terms as the Petrine (Peter) and Johannine (John) paths. The former is concerned with elevating matter into spirit form, and the latter is concerned with infusing matter with spirit. The Sinclairs were in effect carrying both strains of esoteric paths when they worked with the Reshel at Rosslyn, and this would have been a difficult task for their souls to carry.

If you regard the carvings as bearing witness to spiritual truths and patterns then you will start to connect on a deeper level with yourself and the meaning of life and the secrets of creation. Rosslyn's carvings are often seen to represent the third day of creation in the Bible. The carvings are not just depicting Biblical and mythical events – they are also concerned with the ongoing live process of creation for all levels of sentience.

Chapter Two:

Numbers – Their Esoteric Function

There is hidden numerical sequencing in the building of sacred buildings such as Rosslyn. Various forms carved at Rosslyn were associated with the qualities of the cardinal numbers. Numbers were also linked to various nodes within hidden geometric forms in the chapel. The interpretation of numbers belonged to the ancient science of numerology still in use in the early medieval period. Numbers were ascribed individual characteristics/qualities that were in mystical terms expressions of divine frequencies. Another mystical term used throughout this guide is "vibration" to mean a form's frequency that expresses consciousness.

These numbers were not set in isolation but were linked to one another in a divine synergy. The numerological codes at Rosslyn embrace the ancient secrets of creation – the divine was classically expressed in terms of numbers and frequencies of which music as a discipline bears traces yet. These numbers form part of the body of knowledge known as the Reshel that I shall be referring to throughout the book – if we examine ancient Hebrew letters of the Reshel we realize that they were also assigned numbers or vibrationsrelated to spiritual qualities. It appears that through connections made on their travels an inner core of Knights Templar deployed such knowledge in the erecting of the Marian cathedrals throughout Europe, as but one of many projects undertaken. They were a group who were applying ancient inner knowledge en masse to large projects on the ground. They then connected their Gothic wonders to one another by installing patterns of ley lines (earth grids). Such telluric knowledge was preserved through a network of initiates who inherited the secrets, as it was passed down from one generation to another. For instance, Da Vinci understood high alchemical processes very well – his art bears codes that testify to this knowledge.

There are three basic numbers or vibrations that are used as a unified system in spiritual grid work—the 5 (or 10) is a seeding mechanism, the 3 (or 6) is the connective between forms; these are male and female in quality, and the 4 or 8 is the manifesting mode that results as two crosses (cardinal or diagonal). As in general cultural terms, the grid systems too work together as a polarized balance of male and female qualities or functions. The basic generating poles are male (+) and female (-) forming a dualistic couplet. The figures in brackets are essentially the male hidden counterpart form that is only revealed when the female is clarified and restored.

There are other numerical systems. For examples: the "7" (Sheeba) matrix is seen as the "Shekinah", embodying the highest expression of the female and often called the divine feminine. This requires a male seeding complement generally found as the "8th" pole. Since the cathedrals built by the Templars were dedicated to Mary, who was the contemporary equivalent to the Divine Feminine, they encoded their works with a seven vibration by establishing a seven pointed star pattern to connect the cathedrals to one another via a grid. Many of their cathedrals were built on an earth grid of ley lines duplicating the Virgo constellation connecting the cathedrals to one another (One Virgo grid in France uses Mont. St. Michel as the 8th point, correlating with Denebola in Leo.)

The influence of the Reshel on the building of great Gothic cathedrals throughout Europe in honour of the goddess (as key symbol for Creation dynamics) can be evidenced in their designs, and yet none more so than in the tiny example of Rosslyn Chapel.

The references to Hebrew words throughout could appear rather meaningless without a thorough grasp of the sacred meaning of numbers and their correspondent letters. Since there is no accident of design in the intertwining of the ground plan and window designs with ancient sacred Hebrew letters, it is hoped that even for the unskilled a simple explanation taken on trust of the Hebrew link may help in appreciating the design.

William Sinclair seemed to be working with these ancient letters to point toward a higher spiritual science of co-creation as encoded in the Jewish Scriptures. That is why the three monotheistic religions can find so much to relate to in the chapel carvings, as they share the same source material. Working with the hidden geometry of the Reshel and the meanings of the ancient Hebrew letters a series of initiations unfold within the chapel.

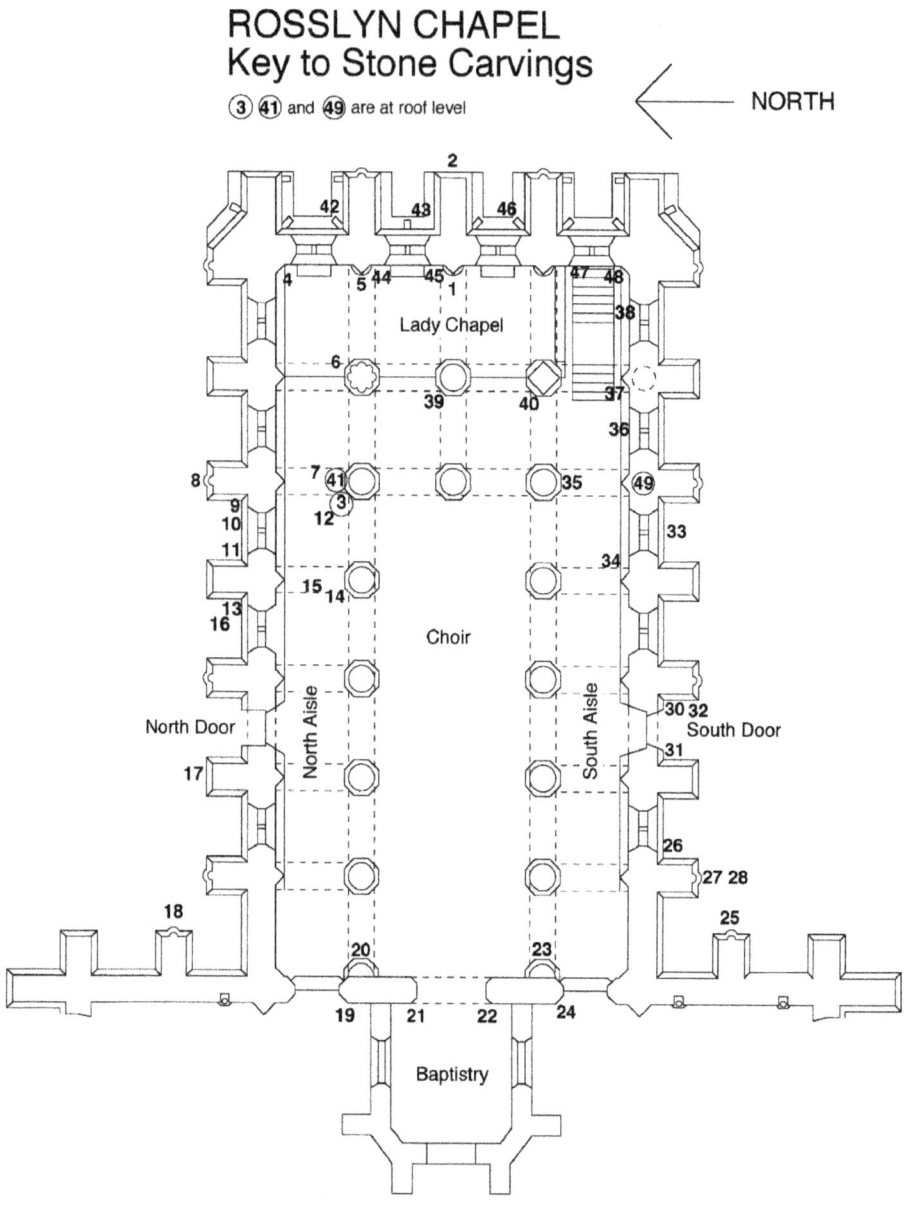

22 • *The Spiritual Meaning of Rosslyn's Carvings*

Chapter Three:

The Central Axis and the Green Ley

It is proper to enter the chapel by the (main) west door rather than the north door that faces the visitor these days. By walking along the central axis you pass a sequence of basic chakras (a name that originated with Indian yoga but has since been used more loosely to describe energy nodes that connect with other nodes in an energy system to create a positive flow of energy when the system is not blocked). As you proceed toward the altar and to the Lady Chapel beyond, many nodes or are passed.

The chapel is oriented true east and so allows for accurate astronomical alignments to occur. The east- west orientation keys into the glen where an extremely significant ley line known as the Sun Line has been discovered. The ley that leads into the glen is acting as a "green ley", linking the chapel with the nature kingdom in the glen below it. The north- south ley known famously now as the Rose Line is the primary ley that utilises the chapel template, and the two main leys intersect within the chapel walls in the Lady Chapel. (The Rose Line is more accurately known esoterically as the Tav Hara Line.)

Addressing the primary east–west axis "green" ley first, this starts outside the Victorian baptistery and continues up the central aisle, through the centre **Journeyman's pillar** bordering the Lady Chapel and out beyond the chapel onto the sloping meadow known as Gardiner's Brae. The ancient ley then continues into a distant clump of Scots Pines that are a devic / elemental gateway to the denser part of the glen's vegetation on the steep slopes beside the river. As mentioned before, the devic frequencies can be felt very keenly in the glen.

From its hilltop position the chapel is linked keenly with the glen where more ancient cultures worshipped via the chapel's central west- east axis. There are said to be at least three major eras when the glen has been a major site of Sun worship – this information is from Maia Nartoomid who has been consciously channelling Thoth for a large part of her life (see *Appendix B* for her contact details – her metaphysical information is very detailed and highly regarded by mystics). Recently scientists from Russia have measured the wave frequencies in the glen in a secret project I was informed of, and their readings showed that the Torshin waves of energy were high – this type of reading is still within the normal range of frequencies but at the very high end of what we can measure. Due to the bowl–like shape of the land here the earth's magnetism is amplified – this may be one of the reasons why lightning strikes are common and plant species regenerate faster and grow taller than elsewhere of a comparable clime and position. The higher level vortices and earth energies do not affect the magnetic field – the Rose Line and Sun Line for instance are high mental or etheric in nature and not measurable with our limited scientific methods.

The chapel harnesses, through intent of design, the high devic forces of nature apparent in the glen, and this green nature kingdom is reflected in the numerous Green Men that have been carved in stone on its walls and bosses. The Green men represent a time when mankind suffered no separation from nature, and the two realms were united in cosmic harmony, as will occur again.

The chapel's carvings are carefully chosen to reflect the energy systems at play–if we look at the **main boss on the central axis** in the Lady Chapel we see it bears a very refined stone carving of a **Green Man (Fig 1)** – one that has been featured in many articles and replicas.

It is no accident that it straddles the point where the central axis of the chapel intersects the Rose Line that traverses the whole length of the Lady Chapel. This king of the Green Men is on the throne of green leys so to speak and it rightfully grins down on us.

Figure 1: *Green Man on boss on central axis Lady Chapel*

Since the chapel's orientation merges with a series of energetic sites in the glen, the chapel becomes the ultimate Green Chapel, with its myriad of plant and nature spirit carvings honouring nature and its innate regenerative properties. On the external wall behind the exquisite Green Man carving lies an ancient **representation of Pan (Fig 2)**, the god of verdant Nature and regeneration. Either side of the carving are the delicate **markings of a chalice**, wrought by the stonemason who carved this wonderful yet worn figure.

Pan appeared in the guise of a goat–headed man, and here we see the god riding what we call the Penta-dove, the dove being one of the three Solarian bird symbols that the inner core of Templars worked with, according to Bill Buehler. A Solarian symbol is one that is set beyond our linear time and is aligned with the central sun of all suns, outside our limited galaxy and within the Metatronic range of frequencies – such knowledge was apparently privy to an inner orders of masons until the early eighteenth century, and their monuments and art evidence this. The Penta or "star" dove is one of the Reshel symbols that represent that affinity with the Metatronic realm, and is resonant with the Sacred Heart of God, and chiefly regarded as the Universal Seed system. According to Buehler, it is also in the exact position that the Reshel geometry dictates, as proof that the Reshel was utilised in the design.

Fig 2: *Pan on central axis, behind external wall*

Pan provides us with a humorous example of how Rosslyn Chapel replicates the Reshel geometry here by placing appropriate symbols at crucial nodes.

Referring to the **cluster of five doves (Fig 2)** below the Pan Figure and the fact that the number 5 represents a universal seeding function, one can say that the Pan is aptly sowing his seeds in the glen by travelling along the Glen ley, first picking up the energy of the Rose Line. Inversely he is feeding the Rose Line with essential green energy. The five doves feed the aforementioned Solarian light codes into the Rose Line here as a seed or initial focal thought form from the wider universe. The Rose Line is at its most potent here because on many levels it is correlating with the "Golden Ratio Point" of a forty mile radius matrix of ley lines.

The Main Window

The main window is centrally placed at the east end of the clerestory level and faces east to receive the incoming morning light, and Venus the Morning Star. This window is the largest and faces over the nave on a key node (the Vau) of the Reshel geometry. The Vau is essentially a 6 vibration found in the apex of an equilateral triangle. There is a strong element of grace infusing this letter. The current pattern formed by the window stone tracery is from the Victorian era yet yields a complex stacking of Hebrew lettering in its design, including the Vau letter. From our earthly perspective we interpret things on a material level, yet many things manifest as a result of initial thought energy. Since the chapel was intended to link with Metatronic energies that cross all boundaries of time as we know it, then the spiritual laws allow the chapel to change or "upgrade" at appropriate times, albeit using human agents. Further developments in the chapel in the near future will result in people entering through the main door facing the main window – this too is a positive development. Returning to the window, the composite layering of letters translates as the Total Regeneration of Earth through the Christ energy. Here is a good example of how a central intent of the chapel manifests in a later phase of building. Outside the Mother and Child can be seen at the bottom right end of the window arch – Jesus here becomes the

Golden Child who regenerates the Earth no less. Unfortunately we can no longer discern what was carved at the other end of the arch.

The Central Axis

When you enter Rosslyn via its main door in the west you pick up the various codes that lie at nodes along its central axis, all of which are carefully amplified by the angles generated from the nodes to the base line. There is a series of geometric rings that centre on a mid point on the base line and pass through the various nodes according to the length of their radii. The rings will pass naturally through the side pillars along each side also, and some freemasons have observed when visiting that the gaps between the pillars are significant. In terms of the Reshel the pillars incorporate the geometry of various sub-systems.

Although appearing simple in design layout the chapel is using ancient geometric codes that were also deployed in the pyramids – it is no accident that there is intense interest shown by the masons whose craft stems from that era.

Chapter Four:

The Circular Route

Rosslyn is a synthesis in many ways of ancient Celtic and Hebrew knowledge systems. Research is now gathering momentum that indicates how in early times in Britain there existed a superior society led by spiritually minded leaders who knew of astronomy and other advanced thinking that in turn influenced the Middle East! The carvings illustrate a rich range of cultures and are used as points of reference to the quest and awakening that mankind pursues through the ages. To assist you identify the carvings all references to them will be in emboldened text.

The Templa Mar and the Northeast

Figure 3: *Letter Shiyn?*

This refers to an energetic system that embraces the eight major directions in order to key into specific spiritual functions of a high heavenly order. Within the eightfold wheel used by the inner core of Templars in what they called the "Templa Mar" format, the northeast is the direction where the heavenly powers of redemption enter the earth's sheaf, and where traditionally the Heel Stone was laid when constructing a building.

Incidentally, both Stonehenge and Chartres Cathedral are oriented to the northeast. In Rosslyn the carvings illustrate an understanding of the dynamic of the Templa Mar. Outside, below the eaves in the northeast corner; the end inscription is a **large ornamental W (Fig 3)**.

The common perception is that this letter is the initial for William St Clair the builder of the chapel, but often on my tours it has had an immediate impact on Jewish visitors who when they look at it perceive it as an ornamental form of their most holy letter Shiyn. One week there were two Jewish families who saw it on separate days with me and the sight of it prompted them on each occasion to a recite:

> "The land we stand upon is sacred
> We will never forsake thee oh Jerusalem."

This invocation to Jerusalem is an interesting coincidence since Rosslyn is supposed to be built on the same ground plan of the original Temple of Solomon in Jerusalem! Christopher Knight and Robert Lomas are key researchers in this area.

The beehive

In addition, until recently an active beehive was functioning in the Lady Chapel. Its entrance was in the very stonework via a flower carving on the northeast pinnacle! **(See Fig 41)** The bees used to exit from an **ornamental ceiling boss** in the northeast corner of the Lady Chapel and circulate harmlessly around the chapel. In medieval times the bee was perceived as a special creature. Buehler calls the bee creature a symbol of the Solarians. The Solarians belong to the Metatronic realm where a central sun of all universes resides. The beating of the Golden Bee's wings matches a particular vibration that is associated with bringing forth Metatronic spiritual humming vibrations into the material plane. The bee embodied the principle of manifesting divine fire codes. By entering literally through a northeast portal these sacred creatures then dispersed the heavenly codes around the chapel. Many of Rosslyn's symbols are aligned with the Sun and other fire codes.

I shall shortly reveal how I perceive a path or journey that begins here in the northeast and culminates over the wide step leading down to the lower chapel. This too correlates with the evidence later revealed by Lomas and Knight in their book the Book of Hiram of how the south aisle of Rosslyn is built over underground passages replicating what exist under the Temple in Jerusalem.

One way to engage with Rosslyn's colossal symbolism is to walk around it in a clockwise direction, starting in the northeast where on a spiritual level the Templa Mar "Heel Stone" energy pole is established. This point introduces the spiritual codes fed into the Chapel's system of rings and 8-point cross. By starting in the northeast so, a journey of the soul starts to unfold.

The North Aisle

The **X cross** in the first window in the north aisle carries Templar symbolism. When you see an "X gram" you assume that the cardinal cross is also there, and together the two orientations of the cross make an 8 pointed cross (Templa Mar) to which the Templars are found to be related. The Druids of the Celts and the holy men within the Amerindians both worshipped the eight directions and ascribed similar energies to them as those which the Templars used in their sacred work. The three cultures were working with the same knowledge as they were able to access the same non-physical dimensions where this knowledge resides.

An X gram is also a shorthand symbol for an inter-dimensional insertion system in terms of spiritual energies. Interestingly for Scotland, the Saltire is an X gram and became the earliest flag in Europe! Its silver blue background indicates that the design carried spiritual light codes, the silver blue representing the Time continuum, which is the

Reshel is known as the Event Horizon. Out of the void all manner of things are created, and the X as a symbol was a powerful manifestation of spiritual light mechanisms on a higher plane.

The X as a theme is repeated more than once here—when we look outside the bases of the outer arch of the north window here, we see that there is a **man holding two scythes crossed** in an X on the left end, and a similar action can be discerned at the other worn end.

There are niches at the bases of this arch- on the right there are **cross bones with skulls atop the two ends**. This is akin to what we see on local gravestones of the early Masonic period (late 17th and early 18th century). Often two heads or faces are carved at the top of the stone, looking in opposite directions. It is a Reshel symbol – the head or skull is the Resh (Chief Head Stone), and when such an image is doubled (or split) we can assume it is of import as a doubling of heads indicates it to be in Reshel mode, meaning a system that uses a Metatronic state of being and function in which Hebrew letters closely describe the form and actions of the system of creation dynamics. The "Reshel" or "Chief Headstone of God" has long been used as a focus in the Hebrew alphabet dynamics and throughout scripture to describe light work, within the Office of Christ as well as the highest archangel Metatron. The two heads probably relate to the archetypal two heads, two faces on one head, split head, two stones/mountains and so forth, that in Reshel terms imply a dynamic that occurs when the two Resh (Chief Head Stone) created poles merge to create a specific "Vault" reality. This would mean that you are linked in with the main Metatronic system used throughout Time for Ascension projects as well as the (Ed: current) transition". The geometry and symbolism used is an expression of divine energies since Rosslyn is concerned with the divine mechanics of creation.

In terms of geomancy (study of the landscape for energetics), a double peaked mountain follows the same Reshel dynamics of the dual or split stone (Resh). The one object (or pole) has become two generating poles, and sets up a creation field in which energy can flow between the two poles created. Throughout the chapel the carvings hint at various "creation vaults" that have been set up for specific spiritual purposes.

The opposite niche is displaying **the Fleur de Lys** motif, identifiable with the Stewart dynasty (and earlier the Merovingian dynasty). The Sinclairs of Rosslyn were staunch supporters of the Stewarts for centuries, and certainly during the time that Rosslyn was constructed. Perhaps the Sinclairs viewed the Stewarts with their peculiar lineage as one of the chosen royal families that could lead the world into a new era of enlightenment. It is as if the Sinclairs were the priests and the Stewarts the kings as in the Celtic times when different families performed royal and priestly roles. We call this the Priest-King dynamic.

The underside of the niche, as with many of them, displays an intricate pattern – in this case there are **six radial ribs in a scalloped base**. The concave shape is mysterious, as it could have been left flat. The scallop shell so created is the motif of both the Knights of St James (who were closely aligned with the Knights Templar) and also was the symbol for a small elite order of just thirteen knights known as the Order of the Cockle, to which William Sinclair belonged.

Figure 4: *Face of Awakening*

The arch itself is graced with **seven large flowers.** Most of the arches display seven flower clusters and seem to honour the devic (nature spirits') kingdom in its most complete form, as seven is the number of the perfected divine feminine.

Now turning to the interior of the chapel and its northeast corner, we can proceed west along the north wall. We begin by looking up in the corner where we can see **a wide startled face** expressing amazement **(Fig 4).** Here in the northeast it is as if a new life of the soul begins.

The carvings indicate that there is a natural progression around the chapel beginning in the northeast, and this face is one of awakening the individual to the journey. It is a journey from the half light back into the full light, or the way from ignorance to enlightenment.

In the first window on the north wall, we have the X gram pattern repeated, with an **angel crossing its hands over its chest**, and the **fleur de Lys** is repeated above the mini temple on the wall.

The Temples

These **miniature temples** are believed to represent the New Jerusalem – one of the themes of Rosslyn is that Jerusalem will be rebuilt, or indeed is rebuilt at Rosslyn. The New Jerusalem represents the state of being attained when one has left behind our half light spectrum of the world of duality and has entered into a heightened state of awareness that accompanies the Full Light Spectrum. According to several inner dimensional teachers there are twenty cycles over aeons of time in which the Earth evolves, to ascend again into the reality from which it fell out of grace – Michael is the main archangel responsible for overseeing us for this cycle (which is our nineteenth phase in the process). The legend of the Fall in many cultures is a reminder of this Fall from grace and the scriptures then reveal in code how to return to the Full Light Spectrum of the higher heavens, under the overall guidance of Metatron the high archangel overseeing the efforts we make.

As with the exterior of the window, there are **seven flowers** in the interior arch – the central flower is divided by a line. In creation dynamics the whole splits into two parts, and this sets up a pattern of creation and individuation until saturation point is met and the cycle of creation begins the long circuitous route back to the indivisible whole. In Reshel dynamics two poles often are set up facing one another to contain a creation field.

Before stepping out of the Lady Chapel we can look up to the ceiling where a centre boss displays the **Nativity Figures** that surround the eight pointed **Star of Bethlehem.** The birth of Jesus is linked with his lineage by the **Lion of Judah (Fig 5)** who looks toward the north aisle from a projecting boss on the east wall.

Figure 5: *The Lion of Judah*

The lion usually indicates that a Gate is being guarded, a Gate" relating to the essential Heart chakra. In the Zodiac Leo is a special sign; the Templars understood that the power of Leo is in the position of the star Denebola. This is the "outer gate" into the higher Metatronic realm and the Sacred Heart (Manifest), or Central Sun of all Central Suns. This "Denebola" position is located at Mont St. Michel relative to one of the Virgo grids in France.

We are about to walk around the chapel, commencing in the northeast corner and walking in the shape of a U or horseshoe we end in the southeast corner where the stairs are situated. The U is an ancient pattern to which stone circles sometimes adhere. An anonymous aviator and experienced dowser once made a fascinating study of Stonehenge, hypothesizing that the inner double horseshoe shape of quartz-rich stones sets up a high charge of negative ions that are conducive for contemplation. He maintained that the doughnut of sandstone creates a sealed system in which the ions build up their conductivity rather than dissipate it. The physical structure of the chapel comes into play here. When we walk between the inner pillars and the external wall–since both pillars and walls are made of sandstone we are in effect walking between two layers of quartz. This dynamic is mirrored incidentally in nature in Roslin Glen below the chapel – the area be comes highly charged with negative ions as the river North Esk gouges a snake-like pattern between the sandstone cliffs in the glen.

The **Master Pillar** borders the inner edge of the aisle as we step down from the Lady Chapel and begin to walk down the aisle – the Master pillar is balanced by the Apprentice pillar in the southeast as the complementary partner pillar bordering the Lady Chapel. In many ways this pillar can be seen as the male of the pair and the Apprentice its female counterpart. In terms of spiritual teaching, the world of polarities is necessary when beginning a journey so that progress can be measured. At higher levels of being the dynamic of polarity ceases to exist, so then themes of Right and wrong become meaningless. At this high level one learns to co-create rather than follow a moral code – needless to say for most mortals the world of polarities is necessary and a stage to recognise and adhere to.

Facing the north aisle on the cross lintel as we leave the Lady Chapel we encounter a **strange letter (Fig 6)** that I would like to play with a little here. It looks like a combination of the Ayin letter with an Aleph crescent inverted on its left end. Ayin is 70 and works closely with its complementary holy letter Aleph (1, 1000) as essential parts of the Creation dynamics. The Aleph letter as a crescent shape is here found to be inverted, and when symbols are inverted there tends to be a higher frequency at play. By inverting the Aleph / Alpha it in effect seals the energies in the system so none of the aspects of Creation can escape – rather like the situation described above with the double layer of sandstone that allows psycho-spiritual energies to build up ad infinitum.

Consider the following example of Buehler's metaphysical work: AYIN (70) means "eye, well" and was drawn as a vesica with a dot in the center. Ayin/An/Anah (correspondent is Ayn/An spelled with Aleph, meaning no-thing) is the AN or divine name ON. An (a) means: *"to eye, pay attention, begin to speak, shout, testify, announce."*

Figure 6: *Ayin Aleph Letter?*

We begin our journey round the chapel paying attention and testifying to the Creator. In Christian terms Christ lived to testify to his father, and the strange letter could also be seen as the Vesica Piscis that represented Christ's temporal life. This would be an apt symbol as the north aisle is concerned with the temporal life of Christ, and the letter is places on its threshold lintel.

Aleph is also closely linked with Resh, a letter that functions as the number nine – it is also perceived as Christ or the Chief Headstone, associated with the northeast here. Nine is also linked to the Ennead and the nine pinnacles above the Lady Chapel testify to the exchange with these angels, and are written at length later in the guide.

The next cross lintel facing us bears the upright and central **Figure of Christ (Fig 7)** who faces the lion of Judah in the Lady Chapel, surrounded by a **chain of four Jewish Scriptures kings** lain at right angles to him either side – since Christ is set at a ninety degree angle to the others, and is upright one can interpret this as Christ representing a major new shift in consciousness. Moreover the new energy or consciousness he bears is superior to the Old kings – he is the new type of King central to them all. The carvings are speaking throughout the chapel of the dynamics of various spiritual energies that interact. Christ manifests a quality of new spiritual energy that is most relevant for our times, even two thousand years on. It is known in the wider spiritual community as Christ energy. Christ is a priest king rather than a secular king. (Many have remarked how the Sinclairs in the historical sense in the fifteenth century bore a similar role with regards to the Scottish kings.)

Figure 7: *Christ as King of Kings / the Priest-King*

Buehler has also suggested that the upright Christ with four horizontal kings beside him is equivalent to the letter Yud depicted as the open hand of an upright thumb with four fingers lain at right angles to it. The Yud is an important pole / letter in the Reshel. The interpretation of this series of carvings as representing Yod/Yud gains weight when we consider that a little further down the aisle we encounter several carvings that symbolise the meaning for the letter Peh. Peh is closely connected to Yod as follows. Yod is the force that connects with all other poles, and is the defining fifth factor that unites the four, for instance in the rivers where Eden is the Yod. Yod can also be the divine breath, connected to the breath that blows in all four corners which is known as the Peh / open mouth. This open mouth is exactly what we see in Figure 13. Further, the open mouth was a symbol defining kingship in ancient Egypt. This ties in with the Christ being recognised as a new king.

Christians who follow the path that Christ exemplified set aside normal everyday affairs and view Christ as their king. For those on the esoteric path, Christ represented their higher consciousness. By inner stillness and meditation one learns to recognise new truths and energies that in everyday life are overlooked. We will return to this theme of kingship later on, when at the end of this journey around the chapel spiritual kingship transmutes to a state of being in truth, which does not need external laws. Truth brings freedom in its wake.

As if to emphasize the contemplative nature of the journey that has just begun as we start in the northeast, outside on the first butt to divide the window bays is an **inverted merman (Fig 8)** clasping his hands over his mouth. He has a tail like the ancient men of Lemuria who lived upon the swampy Earth, or the Fir Bolg, an ancient race of mermen who live on in Irish mythology. Such an evocative Figure is warning us to keep silence and is all the more poignant for appearing so ancient. Here is man at his beginnings in time, with a deep respect for silence. What a long evolution awaits his primitive soul before he is once more at one with the silence!

Above the merman on the underside of another mini temple are two double arches below **a crescent.** The crescent denotes a creation field according to Buehler – and doubling of the arches suggest that there is a high level of spiritual process at play –the same motif can be found on certain early Masonic tombstones.

The right arch outside shows **the devil, or perhaps Pan, snatching a baby** – it is as if to mark that moment when we are born into a world of polarity, of good and evil. At this stage of the journey we are far from perfect and need reminders of the soul battle ahead. The world of polarity is necessary when embarking on a journey so that progress can be measured. However, right and wrong become meaningless when we reach beyond the normal world into a state of very high levels of awareness. Our journey home requires us to find a way beyond polarity, back to the Silence that sustains all. Beyond the duality lies a bliss that belongs to the Shining Ones. The inner path of contemplation will connect us to higher energies to help us discern what is good and what is evil.

Figure 8: *Inverted Merman*

On the inside window arch at each end **angels wear huge garlands or crowns.** The theme of kingship in all realms runs throughout the chapel.

In the ceiling of the first bay in the north aisle we see the **Sinclair cross with a rose in its centre (see Fig 12 on page 45),** while on the cross lintel before we reach the bay we see a cross reference to the **rose in the centre of Christ's chest! (see Figure 7).** The rose links Christ to the Sinclairs and vice versa. It also reminds us of the parallel streams of kinship that seem to exist between the Christ lineage and that of the Sinclairs, on an energetic or soul level rather than at the literal level.

On the right window niche **an angel is crossing his arms over a closed book**, as if sealing the energies for the present, or marking a spiritual stage in life. **An angel is bearing a banner** on the left hand niche – a prevalent symbol in the chapel. Unfortunately any wording that may have been on these banners has long disappeared.

Moving onto the next window, the book that was previously closed is now open – on the inside right niche **an angel is pointing to an open book** under a triple layered round plinth while outside on the outer right arch **a priest–like Figure is holding the book open.** This is all alluding to the opening of seals as we progress down the aisle.

Higher on the interior wall **the Caithness shield** is supported by two men kneeling on either side.

Below the left niche outside lies **a serpent** that culminates in a **falcon (Fig 9),** behind the angel with open book. The Sinclairs sailed from Sinclair Bay in Caithness to Nova Scotia in 1398, and according to Thoth / Maia an "Inverted grail" motif was used by Henry Sinclair on his ship's main mast. If so, the heraldry is appropriately placed here.

Prince Henry was the grandfather of William who designed Rosslyn Chapel, and his expedition is the most obvious explanation as to why Amerindian plants appear throughout the chapel. His "Shamir" Arms as the staff of Aesculapius is shown artistically by Buehler at http://www.shameer-orion.org/pdf/HenrySinclairArms01.pdf

The serpent–bird dynamic as seen in the external carving is equivalent to the "Staff of Aesculapius" dynamic. The earthy raw serpent energy at the base chakra rises to the crown where the Falcon resides.

It indicates an intense opening of the energies here and an initiation taking place. The Eagle is the first of three creatures among the bird kingdom that were seen as Solarian symbols. We have already mentioned the Solarian nature of the bee.

Figure 9: *Bird-Serpent Motif*

According to Buehler "The Solarians use all the sacred birds in one composite dynamic of 'divine principle' we can find in the Hebrew word "abara" which also includes the ability to "cross over, a point of conjunction." This is also included in the Phoenix ascension action. But every bird has its function in the synergic unity; the falcon is a raptor but as a hunter... in the sense that the Messiah is also a "fisher of men" ...the falcon/hawk would relate to the archetypal Holy Child (Horus for the Egyptians) in the Messianic dynamics. The Bird lifts up the Serpent (Shamir) and the two have a gift to the other: The falcon provides the shamir the vision of expanded Messianic perspective: all the Universes are opened. The shamir provides the EXPERIENCE of the vision in an 8-point cross (Templa Mar) along with other systems, by "becoming a diamond." Although the Bald Eagle is primary in the priority of birds, above the Swan and Dove, etc., it is resonant with all the hunters: golden eagle, sea eagle, falcon, owl, heron, et al."

Above the serpent- bird motif at the east of the arch is a **Green Man (Fig 10)** appearing as if in the autumn of his life, his teeth showing gaps and his face looking old. His grin seems to celebrate a breakthrough in consciousness. On the west end of the window arch lays a **large green skull (Fig 11)** hinting of the progression of life from east – west.

The head or skull is the chief symbol for the Resh in Hebrew, meaning Chief Headstone, and was a chief symbol of the inner core of Templars. Inside, directly behind the skull is an angel with the Sinclair cross on a shield under an octagonal triple plinth.

Figure 10: *Green Man in Autumn of Life*   **Figure 11:** *Green Skull*

The Sinclair Cross

Buehler has linked the Sinclair cross with the Resh point in the geometry of the Reshel, so it is interesting that the cross is placed here directly behind the head, or Resh, symbol. There are nine basic poles in the Reshel geometry. The Resh can be regarded as the pole or node in the geometry that synthesizes the functions of all the others. Moreover, within the overall geometry there is a basic cup or grail. At the centre of the elixir filling that cup lies the Resh pole, and this pole drives various pillars that access the Metatronic systems safely – it is this function of the Resh that is at the kernel of its purpose. The Grail is incorporated into the Sinclair heraldry. William Buehler has analysed a coat of arms for Henry Sinclair who sailed to North America, showing the metaphysical Grail angle known as the Bethlehem angle of 26 degrees 18 minutes that he believes governs the arc of each cup on the Sinclair cross. This angle is so called because the angle from the latitude of the Giza plateau to Bethlehem is 26 degrees 18 minutes–this is a very sacred angle and is repeated in the (main) Great Pyramid at Giza where the same angle is formed by the Grand Gallery leading to the King's Chamber.

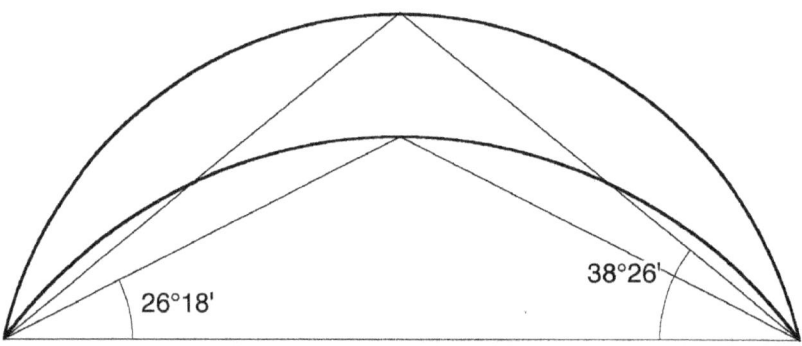

Figure 12b: *The Bethlehem angle.*
(The flatter curve is constructed using an angle of 26°18', while the outer curve closely matches that shown in the Templar Cross in Figure 12a)

William Buehler has slightly altered the Cross to show the Bethlehem Angle forming the "Grail" vesica shape. This appears to be consistent with some early drawings. However the reason Buehler uses the special angle, besides its appearing in the Reshel, is that it is found in notable 'earth' grids; the most dramatic example being the Edinburgh, Glastonbury and Anglesey Head grid where Anglesey Head and Cardigan Bay as a land form display a human Grail figure. Actually the cup in the Reshei forms a number of shapes but the twenty six degrees and thirty minutes is the basic field holding all the rest and is metaphysically more exact. The earth grids referred to are like the Earths "nervous system" that makes it work. Rosslyn Chapel/Castle is in the Resh pole for the Edinburgh Reshei grid but this local grid effects places much further afield – this is described further in my book The Spiritual Purpose of Rosslyn. To summarize, the Resh synthesizes the complete formation of the Grail and the whole Reshel grid.

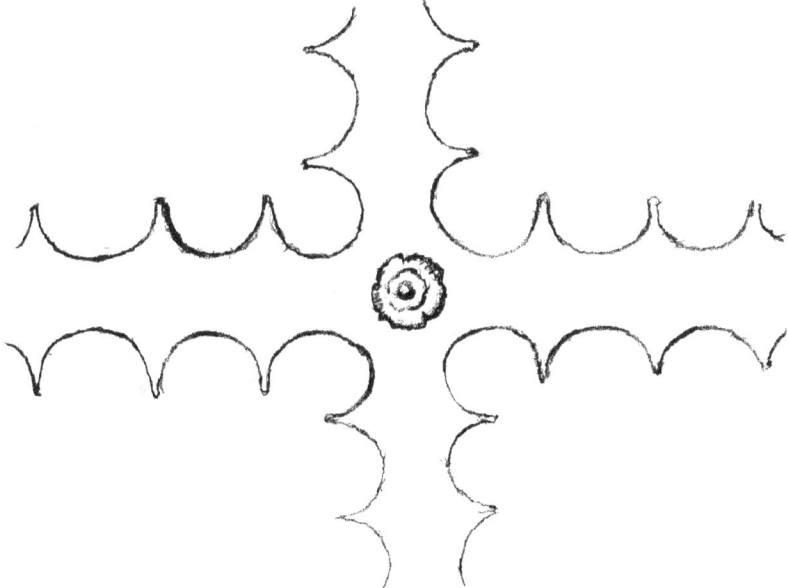

Figure 12a: *Rose in Centre of Engrailed Cross carved in ceiling of side bay*

So not only does the Sinclair shield indicate a strong connection to the Reshel metaphysically, since it was designed for use at Rosslyn which bears a strong telluric connection to many other sites in the world, the shield connects with many souls.

As Buehler says;

> "The shield is an excellent template showing creation-process and the Grail as the main interface between the Selah (Unmanifest and life) and Form, as used in the Reshel."

This means that the shield as a design connects the infinitely creative silence (Hebrew; Selah) with an infinite array of forms.

The Sinclair Cross and Christ Consciousness

The Sinclair cross comprises of an equal armed cross scalloped with eight cups in each direction. These cups are traditionally said to carry Christ's blood as he lay dying on the cross. It is fundamentally a spiritual charge rather than a physical blood line that connects the Sinclairs to Christ. Eight as a number is associated with manifestation codes, so symbolically the Sinclair cross represents Christ consciousness (carried by the blood) manifested in the world. With reference to the legendary meaning of the Sinclair cross, legends often conceal more fundamental spiritual truths that the masses would not be able to receive in the raw. (Similarly the "Grail" was invented as a myth to describe inner states of being that were beyond literal explanation.) Now arguably is the time when the myths and legends can be revealed for what they are in their essence.

The Sinclairs in relation to Christ were fulfilling the spiritual role of (Warrior (King) -Priests to the King; much as, in their temporal world, they fulfilled a similar role for the Stewart Kings. It was a system of mutual support and benefit. In Celtic times certain Druids acted as Priest- Kings, and this continued into early medieval times with certain key families.

In accord with this dynamic, long after the demise of the Stewarts, the Sinclairs are widely studied and recognised at some mysterious level for their destiny.

Another interesting symbol inside is showing **two snakes rising** to meet a pair of wings either side of an external wall butt. This appears to be the same dynamic as the serpent – bird we see under the left niche. It indicates mastery of one's energies so one can fulfil one's destiny. On the inner pillar facing north toward the shield the theme of kingship returns with a **plaited crown or garland of foliage**.

The next window section is dominated by the Hebrew letter Peh, which means an open mouth. First we have on the outer left arch on the external window **a man pulling his mouth wide open** in an exaggerated form, above which is a **Green Man** in a state of sleep.

An angel likewise is drawing his knees up at the opposite end of the arch, above which is **a Green Man** looking quite awake with palms above his head (palms are associated with success and royalty). It is as if the Peh has awakened the Green Man, and indeed the function of the Peh is to create new life form using the sacred breath of life. At the end of most aisle lintels wolf- like beasts spew greenery across the lintel – on the west face of the lintel here **the beast is baring its teeth** in the widest mouth imaginable!

Figure 13: *Open Mouthed (Peh)*

There is also an exaggerated form of a **open mouthed Green Man (Fig 14)**, more crudely carved than usual facing us on top of the inner capital facing northwest... In the proto-Sinaitic glyphs the Peh letter is drawn as a bent tube. While Peh as a letter means various everyday things such as "mouth", "breath", "speech" etc, it can also mean "to blow a wish into four corners". It is the task of the translator to realise the original meaning of the letter within the context of the Reshel. If taken as the latter it is hinting at a powerful form of manifestation. It becomes the Holy Breath of Life and manifestation.

Figure 14: *Peh Green Man*

Immature maize (Fig 15) faces west along the cross lintels here, a motif that is repeated and appears in a far more mature form later. Maize was unknown in the western world at the time. (It was not introduced to Britain until nearly one hundred years later).

At the north end of the lintel, **a tethered wolf or dog** stands upon what appears to be an **alligator,** possibly pulling a blind man. Directly behind on the external wall we have a most unusual stacked motif—below the left window niche is **a man plucking a pheasant** on a fox's back! (Fig 16). It is as if on the inner wall the beast is controlling man while the inverse is true on the outer wall.

Figure 15: *Immature Maize Plant with Crocodile at end*

Returning to the interior, at the south end of the lintel a beast is pulling at the arm of **a crowned harpist.** There seems to be a struggle depicted between the animal and human forces here. In terms of Christ's temporal life, his mission was such that he descended to the earthly kingdom more and more until the time of his crucifixion, and so he was struggling between human and spiritual forces.

Figure 16: *Cook / Pheasant / Fox*

The Templar symbol of the Agnus Dei is on the internal wall boss here, while the inner pillar shows an **elephant** facing east, **a plaited crown** to the west, and snakes once faced south but are too worn to be seen now. In general the nature of the carvings on the inner capitals impart of a sense of victory through the conquering of lower forces and the building of one's inner powers as one passes west–east toward the main altar, culminating in a quality of strength that is traditionally associated with the Master pillar at the end of the row of inner pillars.

The North Door

The north is regarded as the portal into the higher heavens, and is associated with the Father/ Male spirit or energy.

There are **twelve immature maize plants** growing each side of the archway over the door, with **one half formed plant** curling each end from the bottom to the side. The fact that there is a thirteenth plant unfolding is interesting, as according to the mystic community at large the number thirteen is associated with the Ascension of the Earth into a new vibration. The thirteenth zodiacal sign is grounding fast now in the Metatronic realms, and when fully formed it fulfils its purpose by generating a new set of twelve signs as the Earth transcends the old ways: the original twelve transmute into a new set of twelve that comprise the essence of the thirteenth sign. The fact that there are twelve +1 plants shown around the doorway linked with the higher heavens suggests a link to the group of thirteen forming in the higher realms. The plants, normally a south-door symbol, suggest that this door is a "south" door in terms of incoming Spiritual agencies.

There is a wonderful **shamanic Figure (Fig 17)** on the right hand side of the door. His knees are bent and are drawn apart, with a stick tucked behind them. This stick resembles the talking stick that was used by shamans before entering a state of trance in North Amerindian cultures, and more than likely Henry St Clair and other Scotsmen observed sacred ceremonies of the Miqmaqs when they sailed over a few generations before. The shamanic posture is protective as is the foetal position, and it is normal practice to place strong protection at the doorway. He appears to be warning us that we are about to enter other dimensions. His large ears are worth noting too. He who listens knows…

Figure 17: *Shaman with talking stick behind knees*

Close by on the west wall there is **a fierce looking beast (Fig 18)** with large pointed ears and heavy shoulders, and a rope going behind his head that held in both hands. Like the shaman at the north door, he is tucking a talking stick behind his knees.

The crucifixion scene is set to the west side of the north door, also known as the Batchelor Door- the north is associated with the Father or Sky spirit in the Templar / Celtic / Amerindian cosmology while the south is more connected to the Mother and nature processes.

Figure 18: *Shamanic Beast with Talking Stick*

Christ's resurrection is chartered on the inner capitals as you return toward the altar – He appears to be rising from the tomb opposite the crucifixion for instance. One inner capital further east and the **tomb is empty!**

Late eighteenth century guides mention that the pillar on the north wall opposite the crucifixion scene (at time of descent from the cross) depicted John and Mary looking across, although the Victorian Episcopalian guides says there were three women and that there may have been those who were close to Jesus facing the scene of his death. Mary Magdalene, Mary the mother of James and Joses, and Salome the wife of Zebedee. An **angel bears a crucifix form** on the niche below the Crucifixion scene.

Directly opposite in the left window arch the **same devil–like creature** that was shown snatching a babe further back outside, is now **tempting an adolescent** whose mother is shields him. Once more we can see a maturation or development in the symbols, reflecting the metaphysical journey taking place.

This is the last window on the north side and has **nine rather than seven flowers** in its archway, and no angels. Seeing nine as the number of completion, it is fitting that Christ's journey has ended in this aisle.

It is almost as though the whole of the north aisle is concerned with the descent of man into matter which facilitated a conquering of the lower forces experienced during this necessary fall from the heavens. Outside on the lower left of the external window there are **two rams facing head-head** with a beautiful tree growing behind them in the middle. This suggests that the forces are coming into balance. Opposite on the right there is **a man riding an open – mouthed beast** who is turning his head back to face the man. Man and beast are working together here. **Simple green men** are in the upper arches outside, resembling seed pods.

The West End

If we started in Autumn in the east and have travelled through winter, we are reaching the early stages of Spring, when the seeds are quickening again. The area beyond the last window on the north wall is flanked by an inner pillar only.

There is no window in this area, and so we will look at the interior here only. The inner capital is interesting – facing west **a man is either feeding or struggling with a swine or boar.** Victorian Christians deciphered it as the prodigal son feeding the swine, although we need to be cautious here – the Victorians were recreating a church and accompanied this with a guide – so they tended to translate the carvings according to a rather narrow set of criteria. Rosslyn is multi-layered and also truly multi-cultural, so it is wiser to look for signs according to more than one faith. For instance, followers of Arthurian mythology and Celtic legends may identify the carving in question as the white sow Hen Wen, a form of Cerridwen the Goddess symbol who tried to feed her son Avagddu with a wisdom-inducing magic potion, but whose other son stole the first vital three drops. He eventually was reborn as Talieson the bard. Avagddu meanwhile died of the poison that the portion yielded after the first three drops were taken. Given that we are close to another Celtic symbol **(see Fig 20)** this may be another Celtic reference.

Stone references to Christ abound at Rosslyn and seem to generate a sense that He was the Christ energy available for all to ultimately experience. It may be more important to see the pattern developing rather than isolating each stone and labelling it. Everything is connected to the other and the carvings cannot be taken in isolation – their positioning seems to sets up a highly developed system of harmonics that very rarely is noted in our mundane world. Only through developing one's inner senses could such connections be made on a conscious enough level to design the carvings as lain out at Rosslyn. Whoever orchestrated the whole design was a remarkably awakened individual.

Facing east on the inner pillar are **two doves with foliage** – the dove is one of the Solarian birds in Reshel cosmology and is associated with a past, present and future time continua. The future continuum carries a far brighter light, to which we will transition when consciousness en masse rises to a sufficient extent. There will be those of higher vibrations whose wisdom and love will support other sectors of humanity to ascend too. This ascension process for humanity is not necessarily anything catastrophic but will occur in the spiritual realms primarily and will gradually affect the physical world we live in. At present we are straddling our present temporal continuum with its concurrent range of dimensions, and the future one that we are rapidly "upgrading" to – this means the dimensions are frequently shifting grounds in our present continuum.

Returning to the **inner pillar** in this area, there are **other birds on the other sides**- on the south side they appear to be feeding one another – or at least crossing their beaks. On the north side their wings are crossing. An X gram in the bird kingdom indicates a dimensional shift, and birds are traditionally associated with the head and crown chakras. Perhaps by starting with Christ's birth and the birthing process in the east, the lower chakras associated with birth give rise to the higher chakras in the west. The dimensional shift (X gram) is common to all chakras and so is repeated in many motifs in the chapel.

The protruding west wall here was reputedly intended to be part of a side nave that never was completed. On its west side is the rough outline of a side altar and also a piscine and aumbry. If you look at where the continuation of the nave would be, it appears like a crumbling wall. The wall ends are held together by roughcast harling. The skilled eyes of stonemasons are able to note here that the wall was constructed from its foundations to appear unfinished, so proving the original intent was to leave the chapel in an unfinished state. The west wall does not support the building and is merely decorative and according to Lomas and Knight (The Book of Hiram by Lomas and Knight, Arrow Books 2004) the wall mirrors the layout of the original Jerusalem temple ruins, otherwise known as the Wailing Wall. The story runs that William Sinclair over-ran his budget and was forced to build only the choir area, despite having spent six–eight years on the foundations and twenty six years on the building above the ground, and having to import masons from abroad whom he promised disproportionately life – long high salaries. Given his apparent high level of intelligence and connections within European noble circles it is unlikely that he would have underestimated the time and budget to this extent – the siting and fabric of the wall suggests they were deliberately building a small building that echoed the proportions of Solomon's temple and no more. This has prompted freemasons to regard the unfinished wings of the west wall as duplicating the old wall of Jerusalem.

Inside the chapel on the west wall we have a **Caithness memorial to the Sinclairs,** lying against a bricked in doorway. Its symbols include the coat of arms bearing the galleys that sailed to Nova Scotia pre-Columba, and the globe artichokes that the Knights Templar revered. The chapel was used as a burial ground for the owners in its interim years as a ruin. It is interesting to note that the present chapel has not been an active church as long as its predecessor downhill in the present cemetery area, and that the current chapel has spent less time as an active chapel than as a ruin! The small burial marker stone to the right below is dated circa 1337 and is not in its original position because it was discovered outside the chapel – but its pattern has been analysed for Reshel features by Buehler who believes it to be a pattern of an earth grid linked with stewardship of the land, in close allegiance no doubt with the Stewarts who they outwardly served and whose name originally meant Stewards of the Land. This can be viewed at

http://www.shameer-orion.org/pdf/WmSinnclaerTombL.pdf

There appears to have been a mutual support system between the Stewarts and the Sinclairs, with the Sinclairs fulfilling an equivalent role of the Celtic priest advisor to the temporal kings– Mary of Guise in her letter to Earl Sinclair at Rosslyn in 1546 shows remarkable respect toward him.

Outside here on the extreme left of the lintel, above the blocked left doorway, we see **a hand holding curly kale.** This is a symbol of regeneration in the plant kingdom and ties in with a Figure at the opposite extreme end of the lintel.

Three large sunflowers span the lintel across the blocked left doorway that leads to the extreme right end of the lintel, where there is **a Figure tied to a rock with a beast pecking at its side(Fig 19).** This strongly resembles Prometheus the Fire god who awoke each morning renewed, despite dying every night as the beast pecked away his liver. The theme of perpetual regeneration is one of the key themes of the chapel so the placement of this mythical Figure just to the left of the main doorway is apt. The Victorians added a baptistry here that conceals the main entrance.

Figure 19: *Prometheus*

This strong symbol of regeneration among the gods is matched by an image on the interior at the top of the pillar of **two dragons intertwined (Fig 20)** – an ancient Druid symbol for the balance between the masculine and feminine energies. When there is harmony in their relationship, power can manifest. For example, each chakra has masculine and feminine energies, and both have to be balanced for the chakra to function properly. As with the X formations, the double dragon is a portent for new manifestations to occur. As in many of the carvings at Rosslyn, the dual worlds of gods/ angels and elementals/ mythical beasts are combined on one spot, albeit with a wall between them. The dragon or serpent is one of the many recurring symbols seen in Rosslyn. Christ can be seen as the Serpent who has mastered all levels. His temporal life started in the east end of the chapel with his birth, and he has completed it with victory over life in the west. Having seen beasts in conflict all the way along the west faces of the inner capitals, there now is a resolution. There is no separation between older religious themes of renewal and Christ's message of renewal. In man, his lower nature is subdued by allowing the higher forces to reign supreme, so that a new inner freedom is gained that brings peace and understanding in its wake. Now in the opposite (south) aisle the journey of initiations is about to begin for man, Christ having paved the way for humanity to follow the same path of awareness, and walk in the light of a much higher order than normally contemplated.

Figure 20: *Interwining Dragons*

The central theme of regeneration will continue up the south aisle. The mastering of basic impulses in the north aisle precedes mastering the inner path of self – regeneration in the south aisle.

On the internal wall to the right of the door is the mark of a **crude equal armed cross** that was typical of the early Jerusalem crosses, and could have been executed by a Portuguese mason. The Templars became the Knights of Christ in Portugal, and there is a close connection between Portuguese masons and the ancient Templars. In current times the masons in Portugal still call Rosslyn their Portuguese chapel abroad! As far away as the Armenian Church in Jerusalem, Rosslyn has been known of for centuries, for its carvings also embrace Coptic knowledge of the angels. The main theme of the chapel is as a Green Chapel to honour regeneration, but as a system looking at the forces behind creation it will inevitably include the role of the angels in its plan. The historic links with the Middle East forged during the Crusades, in particular with the Sufi strain of Islamic mysticism, helped the understanding of the angelic realms.

The Main Door

If we stand in the Victorian baptistery and gaze at the main door, we can just make out two much worn **green men** at the pillarbases either side, with **sunflowers and other flowers** above. The top right bears **a Fleur de Lys (Fig 22),** the symbol of the Steward dynasty but in fact a far more ancient French symbol and also the logo for the ancient god of architecture Thoth) while the top left bears **a trillium plant (Fig 21)** that belonged then to the New World only. However Christopher Columbus did not reach there until many years later, so we can assume that this is another plant seen during the 1398 voyage. The Sinclairs have never forgotten the deep respect the Amerindians showed for Prince Henry who orchestrated the voyage to Nova Scotia. By all accounts the Miqmaq Indians have not forgotten either.

The main door is crowned then with plants from the Old and New World. These two plants were adopted as provincial plant symbols for Ontario and Quebec in Canada. This is a clue to the voyage made in

1398; as Buehler says, these men were seeding North America with a (Reshel) ley pattern that already had been utilised in Europe. By inward intent they were extending the Reshel leys over this new land that they knew would be inhabited by Westerners in the near future. Their intent as indicated by the ley lines was that the land be governed according to the "as above so below" Principle. It was no accident that Washington was founded by freemasons whose knowledge stemmed from Templar times when the Reshel was in sharp focus and applied within a powerful and large group.

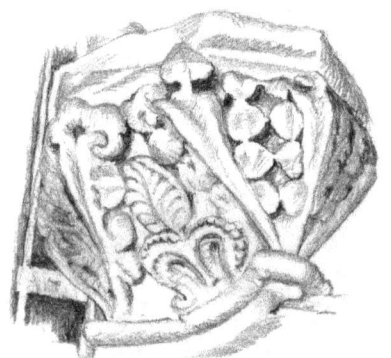 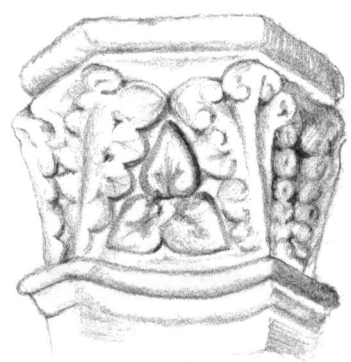

Figure 21: *Trillium*   **Figure 22:** *Fleur de Lys*

To the right of the main door there is the other side entrance that is blocked. At the top of the exterior main side pillar, a **figure in medieval attire** is more than likely William St Clair who built the chapel. In earlier guides there is mention that the Figure was carrying a child, but the carving of the child has worn away. The Victorians were of the opinion that this was St Christopher, but given the manner in which the Figure is clothed, and the fact that directly behind this carving is another carving generally taken to be William St Clair in his old age, it is far more likely to be William carrying the Christ child. He is regenerating humanity with the Christ energy. Directly inside the wall on top of a pillar **William Sinclair stares out, crowned and bearing a sword**. He is both priest-king as in the ancient Celtic and Hebrew tradition, and warrior-priest too. The roles were interchangeable.

High above him on the wall another **younger face** stares down that is generally known as the Apprentice. Earlier last century this face used to display a beard, but it was chipped off leaving a mark on the wall where the chipping instrument struck. Apprentices were not allowed to grow beards so this probably explains the removal of the beard, in order that the Apprentice myth could be borne out in stone. The gash on the forehead is reminiscent of Hiram Abif who suffered a similar blow to the head whilst building the first temple of Jerusalem. There is a powerful parallel between William St Clair as architect of Rosslyn and Hiram Abif as chief builder of the Temple in Jerusalem. Rosslyn's layout mirrors the earlier versions of the temple in Jerusalem, and at the time when William Sinclair's ancestors partook in the Crusades the idea had grown of rebuilding the temple in Jerusalem. This dream had to be abandoned due to Muslim occupation. In many ways Rosslyn can be seen as the alternative location for the New Jerusalem temple that the Crusaders hoped to create. The younger face known as the Apprentice is actually William in his youth, while the lower one shows him when his life is spent, having dedicated much of it to constructing the chapel.

Figure 23: *The Three Cockle Shells*

William approved templates of each carving in Norwegian landsmaar (high quality pine) wood before he had the pieces carved in stone. There is said to be a layer of crushed cockle shells between the individual carvings and stones as part of the general mortar / binding material. On the west wall, level with the top of the same capital which bears his aging head are three large and **prominent cockle shells (Fig 23).** According to legend William was a Knight of the Cockle, a prestigious Europe-wide order that had only 13 members in his day.

This carving faces the inner row of pillars on the south aisle. As remarked a little earlier and noted by others over the years, the north aisle is focussed on Jesus Christ, while there are more references in the south aisle to the Sinclairs. This would reflect the dynamic of the priest–king, both Christ and the Sinclairs being in similar priest-king roles. Christ was concerned with bringing Heaven on Earth through his teachings, while the Sinclairs when serving the Stewart kings hoped to influence temporal affairs with divine providence. Since blood carries the essence of a person, the Sinclairs bear the essence of Christ in the cups of their engrailed cross, and their understanding of his spiritual heritage is reflected in the carvings. It is as if the Sinclairs were extending the priestly role into the earthly plane when they became the cup-bearers to the Scottish king from the eleventh century. While the Stewarts were but temporal creatures of rule, the Sinclairs as a clan often appear to have been a type of longer-term spiritual ruler, advising the kings on their affairs. Within Scottish history the Sinclairs were close advisors to the Scottish kings during the six-generation Stewart Dynasty. Legends say they were relied upon as second to none and consulted in all matters.

Directly behind this carving on the outer west wall around a capital a line of **rhombic structures** surround **single roses (Fig 24).** These are to the adjacent right of William Sinclair holding the Christ child, and appear strangely Masonic to many who behold them. The rose seems to connect with the Christ energy, while the rhombus as a symbol in the Reshel reflects higher energies.

In Reshel geometry the rhombus is seen as a portal into very high energies. A high level of awareness would befit William's role and function in building this chapel and his close juxtaposition to the rhombi seems fitting. On the right end of the doorway there is **a hand holding acanthus leaves,** symmetrically placed to match that other plant revered by the Templars at the left hand side of the entrance: curly kale.

Figure 24: *Rhombus and Roses*

Inside, behind this image **a man is holding a large stem of a plant** that almost swamps him and which seems to grow out his own body! This hidden image epitomises one of the main missions of the chapel, which is to realign humanity harmonically with nature, and to regenerate in all kingdoms. So, although obscured by an oversized later baptistery, either side of the main door we have plants and figures connected with the forces of regeneration: Prometheus the god to the right and William the man to the left. While Christ and Prometheus can be seen as figures who mastered individual self – regeneration, William's path on the right side here is more concerned with a collective regeneration of Scottish culture. When designing the chapel he integrated the Reshel into its layout. The Reshel is chiefly concerned with the mysteries of Creation and so the dynamics of regeneration are represented. As chief builder of a chapel whose carvings express the regeneration of many sentient forms of life, the hidden geometry hints at a process whereby Heaven is created on Earth. The Reshel as a spiritual light system has been used by many generations of mystery schools. The Templars were the last group en masse to use the knowledge. Jesus Christ understood the art of masonry or building too, and Rosslyn used this medium to express a deep affiliation with Christic mysteries.

Turning to the south side, on the east–facing side of the west wall, there is a buttress below which there is a well–concealed carving of **Hiram Abif (Fig 25)**. The gash is very evident on his forehead and his thick strands of hair are like downward pointing crescent horns – this contrasts with the angels and other Figures inside the chapel who have their hair turned upward in the shape of crescent horns. The crescent in Reshel terms is a creation field and pointing down toward the ground may mean that there is a Spirit to Matter process at play here. We are now on the south side of the chapel and the south is traditionally associated with the elemental or nature kingdom. Interestingly the Hiram Figure is in the same position as the griffin with talking stick and large ears on the north wing of the west wall.

On a parallel with Hiram on the west wall inside are the two afore-mentioned depictions of William Sinclair at different stages of his life. Like their counterpart carving above the inside capital beside him, **cockle shells** cluster to form open-mouthed flowers **around the inner arch** in the window. On the internal wall at the top of a pillar stands **a sheaf of corn** among foliage. The sheaf seems to denote a first harvesting, and the theme of harvesting continues later in this aisle. The whole of this aisle seems concerned with a series of initiations, starting here in the southwest. The efforts of inner work are yielding spiritual harvests.

The South Aisle

The first degree of initiation in freemasonry is shown in the left niche at the base of the window arch – **the blindfold man, kneeling, is held in a loose noose led by another (Fig 26).** There is a legend which speaks of how twelve local families met in the lower chapel that formed part of the Norman castle which stood where the chapel now stands. They refused to move to the new castle built in the early fourteenth century. The ideas expressed in the carvings at Rosslyn originated locally with an inner core of Templars who lived on estates in the vicinity of the chapel

Figure 25: *Hiram Abif*

and who used the lower chapel for ceremonies even long after their organisation was officially disbanded – the knowledge did not disappear. The Scottish lodges are allegedly the oldest in the world and incorporated the roots of a mystery school tradition into their early initiation ceremonies, some of which remain and can be recognised at Rosslyn. Many of these initiations expressed in the stone carvings here probably go unrecognised, as by the mid eighteen century freemasonry appears to have lost its direct inner gnosis with a sacred tradition practised by the inner Templars Directly inside the Hiram, right of the window niche **an angel is protecting the kneeling man** who appears to have markings around his neck – this is a rather obvious case of the inner and the outer walls expressing the same phenomena. As mentioned earlier, all along the south aisle we are concerned with a series of initiations that culminate at the juncture of the steps leading down to the lower chapel.

Figure 26: *Initiation Rite*

The idea of initiations has also been linked to ground scanning exercises in Rosslyn that echo the Jerusalem temple layout. According to Niven Sinclair it is here that tunnels enter beneath the chapel and run along the south aisle as far as the altar, much the same way as they do in Jerusalem's ancient subterranean system of tunnels. Stability checks using excavating machinery in recent years did not unearth any of the fabled sand–filled extended vaults. Even so, the Victorian idea is effectively suggesting that the chapel is showing above ground what is recorded in the Jewish Scriptures, while its underground foundations is mirroring a future temple of Jerusalem as written in the Book of Revelation. This very thought creates a way of thinking that is in line with the Reshel that presupposes events manifest in all three time continua simultaneously. The power of thoughts cannot be underestimated in creating new realities.

On the interior here the two mini temples both have **six pointed wheels** under their bases. Many of the mini temples display intricate designs under their bases.

The window has **nine flower clusters** that on closer examination **are fourfold Fleur de Lys** facing inward and forming a diagonal cross. This may be a shorthand expression of the eight-sev pointed wheel and the use of the Fleur de Lys hints again at the connection between the Merovingian kings, the Egyptian god of architecture and the Reshel knowledge.

Outside there is a mini temple below which **an eight-pointed wheel** emanates from a seed pod. Beyond the pod lies **a Christ-like Figure** under the end of a projection. See **Fig 27.**

Fig 27: *8 pointed wheel under temple external boss*

Assuming it is Christ, could it be placed here because Christ too knew the secrets of architecture as a means to expressing divine mysteries of creation, an essential Jewish theme? The building of the temple of Jerusalem is a major theme in this corner, and in fact a little further up the aisle the presentation of Jesus in the temple is carved on a capital, although this is too worn to decipher nowadays. When Jesus was questioned he could have talked among other things of the secrets of the building of the temple, as his father Joseph was no ordinary carpenter but from a noble family.

Figure 28: *Feather Grouping*

On the outside of the window below a niche there are **some feathers (fig 28)** like those an Indian squaw would wear. The spine of a feather equates with a lightning strike in initiation rites. It is as if the equivalent rite of passage in the Amerindian culture is honoured here – could it be that some of those on the 1398 voyage from Sinclair Bay in Caithness partook in Miqmaq initiations?

Returning inside, the first capital on the south side used to show a group of carpenters / stonemasons facing the angel / first degree initiate. Among the group is a larger central unknown Figure. Perhaps the central Figure now worn represents their Grand Master observing the rite? The north side of the capital has **a large Green Man with palms** (indicating victory or mastery) from his mouth, and **a seven-leafed aureole** surrounds the first disciple above him in the arch. The inner arch faces north, with the twelve apostles and four others, all with nimbuses. **St Andrew** is shown with the diagonal cross on which he was crucified–another X symbol. **St Bartholomew** / Bart or Nathan is beside a fig tree. The disciples were initiated into the Christic mysteries. Taking the other symbols in this area into account, some of the Templars were likewise initiated at Rosslyn.

On the inside right window niche **Queen Margaret (Fig 29)** is holding a portion of **the "true" cross** – her family is said to have retained this holy relic which she brought with her to Scotland. **Her hair** is upturned in the crescent / Moon/ cup shape that reflect the ancient form of the letter Aleph which is associated with setting up a creation field. This depiction of the queen, who was a patron saint of the St Clairs, suggests she was bearing and creating a new set of codes to live by, and that on a soul level she was highly evolved. She is borne on a horse by William the Seemly. (Moreover the horse in the Reshel energy system marks out an energy and consciousness function wherein a temporal creation field is created – this would accompany the meaning of the crescent shaped hair on the rider well). Her family were Ironsides of early English high nobility, and her grandfather is buried at Glastonbury Abbey. When her brother's position as close contender for the English throne was not honoured her own standing was not settled, and yet she was unprecedentedly supported and protected by noble families in Hungary and other places in Europe. Some Masonic research declares that there were key families in Europe that shared a common access to ancient knowledge of initiation. It is very likely that Margaret belonged to one of these families, and so she was offered protection in her travails in Europe. It is interesting that often heraldry of early Norman – Celto Scottish families bears a close resemblance to the Reshel symbols. Above all,

Queen Margaret was a staunch supporter of the ancient group of early Christians known as the Culdees in Scotland, and it was through this enigmatic group that much of the old Druid love of nature was integrated into the early Christian church here, which in turn paved the way for places like Rosslyn to emerge. There would have been a network in Scotland of Culdee-influenced Celtic nobles who kept their lands and lived alongside the Norman settlers, and whose belief systems quite naturally influenced the development of the medieval church in Scotland. She was sanctified for her acts of piety in Scotland and she converted her husband King Malcolm Canmore to peaceful Christian ways according to the tales that survive.

Figure 29: *Saint Margaret with cross*

The cross lintel just before the south door has some other form of **sacred Amerindian succulent** on its east face. Some believe it is Aloe Vera, others say tobacco. As all the plants are stylised it is hard to identify them for sure. If it is indeed tobacco, this could be marking the sacredness of a portal or initiation as tobacco is commonly used as a peace offering to the gods at holy sites or during holy ceremonies. At its south end just to the right of the doorway are the remains of what once was the **Presentation of Jesus in the temple of Solomon**. Was Jesus initiated during this time away from his parents? It would appear so, and that the builders of Rosslyn knew so. Were the Sinclairs at the time Rosslyn was built aware of a lineage of knowledge stemming from Solomon that Jesus, too, was part of?

At the other end of the lintel, the second inner capital facing south shows a **Figure kneeling in prayer** and facing the scene of presentation (Anna prophetess Luke II:36?) Many of the carvings on this and the following inner capital are too worn to make out but were a mixture of humans and animals. The carvings taken as a whole do suggest that Christ received his first degree of initiation in the temple when he was twelve years of age.

The north side of the inner capital shows **a lion and unicorn** fighting. To the west side is **a lion** and the east **a wolf** that appears tethered. These animals are hard to decipher and are very often found at the tops of the inner capitals, as if representing some form of internal conflict.

The South doorway

On the left hand side we see a **large-eared crouching man** who is a worn version of the similar shamanic figure that lies directly across at the north door.

The green men in the arch of the doorway are rather worn creatures, with most of the foliage gone around the arch, but there is a splendid **inverted Green Man (Fig 30)** on the right hand side – this is the only inverted Green Man in the chapel.

Universal among cultures whose cosmologies align with deep truths, the south direction represents the portal into the elemental kingdom—the inversion here of the Green Man denotes the significance and function of the south. As with the inverted web-footed men on the north and east external walls, the inversion draws attention to their symbolism. When inverted the energy related to that symbol is of a higher frequency than normal — it represents a higher reality beyond the normal linear appearance.

Figure 30: *Inverted Green Man*

The energy / consciousness of that image is now set in a freer dynamic where there is a two- way flow. Normally we only perceive an image or a flow of energy as one way. When dowsing sites as powerful as Rosslyn, there are dowsers who can access the higher energy spectrums of the Reshel it links with, and perceive that their pendulums are rotating one way when in fact to an observer they are rotating in the opposite direction.

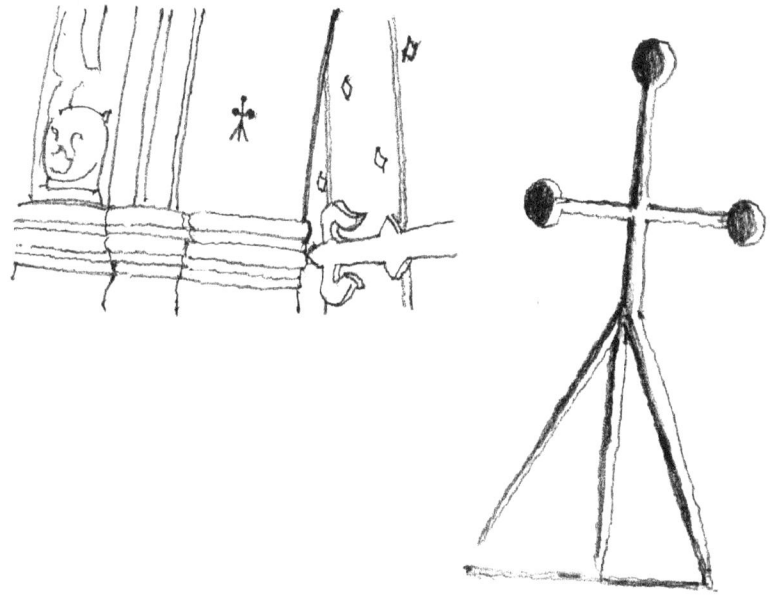

Figure 31: *Mason's Mark in left hand arch South Door*

In Catholic times the congregation used this door to enter by when coming from Rosslyn castle. After about a hundred years the chapel was in disuse, and remained so for nearly three hundred years. The door was known as the Women's Door not because only women could enter through it but because the women were known to be more bound by tradition to the earth mysteries and its "lower heavens", and the south was the direction aligned with the spiritual mother and nature. Similarly the north was perceived as the domain of the spiritual father, and it was a male function to connect with the higher heavens so the north door was known as the Batchelor's Door. One of the main functions of the chapel is to reflect and honour the high energies of the Nature kingdom, and as a green chapel it sought to reunite mankind with nature. The next thing to note in the doorway is the most **delicately executed mason's mark (Fig 31)** on the inner left arch – this mark is repeated in the north doorway and in the small yet significant room to the north side of the lower chapel. By marking these three key areas the mason is associated with the male and female halves of the expanded Goddess and a single seed in the Christic half. The upper chapel is essentially female (Shekinah/Goddess) in quality while the lower section is the male (Christic) half of the Reshel.

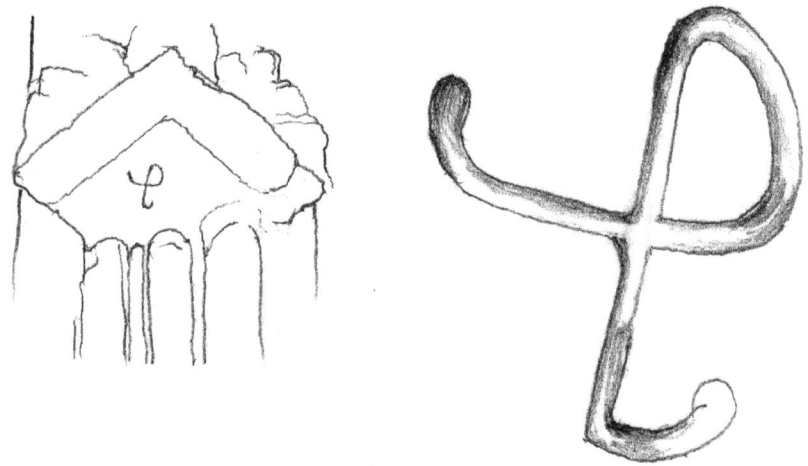

Figure 32: *Mason's Mar on right of South Door*

There is **a mason's mark like a fish (Fig 32)** on the upper right side of the doorway, and this looks like a smaller version of the inscription on the first lintel leading off the Lady Chapel, without the inverted crescent capping one end. The external walls display original mason's marks while on the interior that was coated with thin cement in the twentieth century, the mason's marks may be much later.

Inside the doorway the left hand pillar is capped by a group representing **the Annunciation of the Virgin group** in an aureole, according to older guides. The only thing that still can be deciphered is perceived as the **Mandylion of Veronica**, who received an image of Jesus on the cloth she wiped his face with during the time of his passion. The stone has been tampered with according to historians. There were a number of scenes from the Passion of Christ at this position either side of the chapel. The archway above the doorway like that in the north side has two layers—The outer arch has **21 flowers of three-leafed curly kale** and the inner arch has 10 flowers with many more on its base that are hidden.

To the right of the doorway outside there is an atypical low buttress with **a Figure bound between poles,** holding a continuous plant in either hand. Under the left window niche is a **two-humped camel.** The camels would have been encountered on the Silk trading routes. In the left outer arch of the window is **a goat or ram** while in the right arch stands **an eagle.** The right niche carries a **griffin** while the butt to the right has a **female Figure** with her hair flying out. There is a sense of growing power in the symbols used.

High above the left arch of the external window a **dragon's tail** swirls upwards from a human Figure. Inside a **double-stacked head of a snake** rests ominously on one of the two abnormally angular plinths either end of the window arch, at the right end of the arch. On the left end the foliage forms an evocative image of **two hands coming together in prayer.**

The interior has **nine palms** in its archway – again a sign of victory or power.

The Green Man at the bottom left of the arch appears older than further down the aisle, while the right hand base has a **Green Lady,** looking a lot younger. It is as if the male energies are decreasing and the female increasing in the south aisle leading east. There are green ladies along the south aisle with their more traditional counterpart green men; the ladies just wear the garlands of greenery on their heads. Since the south is associated with the female energies and nature it seems fitting to find the green ladies here. It is interesting that, overall, more women are carved in the south aisle.

Facing north on top of the inner pillar there is a large **square-headed Green Man** showing a few teeth. There are two **tiny green men linked by a worn garland** on the south side of the pillar. It is as if the green (elemental) energy enters from the south and sets up a current that is grounded at the pillar with the two green men who create a containment field for the energy – the energy then manifests beyond them in the form of a large single Green Man, as the energy flows into the nave of the chapel and its central axis. The cross lintel has a **chain of small hearts** decorating it. The energy here seems to be about higher green energies, and the power of love.

The carvings on the external wall are worn but in the next window arch we can see a **host of nine green kings and possibly green queens** (**Fig 33**) also in regal poses – wearing **crowns of greenery** on their heads. The central Figure seems to be holding a sphere, and has two other heads on his/ her shoulders!

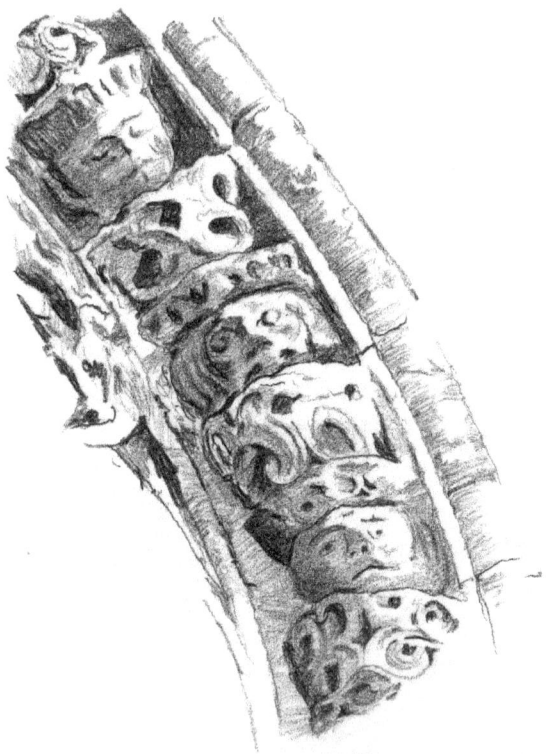

Figure 33: *Green Grail Monarchs*

On the right hand base niche there is a fascinating **figure holding a vessel between his knees.** The inside window arch is decorated with a **host of nine angels** that mirror their green counterparts outside. The capital on the inner pillar here is decorated with **palm fronds**. To the west a hand holds two fronds that are opening, while to the east an arm is holding a single large open palm leaf. This is similar to how the green men on the pillar further back developed a pattern where the two poles (hands) set up the field and the larger single motif manifests on the other side as a result.

The exterior carvings are too worn to decipher as we proceed east. The interior now becomes far busier with motifs, as we seem to reach the stage of another initiation, the preparatory ground work having been done at the start of the south aisle. The plant kingdom has been moving toward summer and its harvest. There are no flowers in the window arch here—instead as mentioned above there are **nine angels all holding scrolls.** Here the angels are honoured rather than the nature beings (elementals). They prepare the way with divine messages or codes. If we could read the banners the angels bear throughout the chapel we might understand more of the message within.

On the right base **Moses** is wearing **a large crescent on his head (Fig 34).** He is a key Figure in the Jewish Scriptures whose passages reveal Reshel light codes. The significance of his soul is marked with this crescent /Reshel letter Aleph, first letter in this ancient sacred Hebrew alphabet. In terms of the Reshel Moses represents the secular aspect of Yahweh, so it is fitting he is sited in the (Sinclair/ human) southern aisle as opposed to the Christ aisle in the north. It is interesting that both Moses and William Sinclair are representing secular aspects of God. Moses carries the tables of stone upon which God's commandments were written – the sacred words he was entrusted with. Moses was a master soul who altered the path of mankind, and in effect bore the seeds of a new consciousness for humanity. William Sinclair by contrast was occupied with building a temple that expressed the divine aspects of truth. Any initiate on a path of enlightenment will affect the state of consciousness of his world and those around him through his own efforts.

Figure 34: *Moses*

On opposite left base is **an angel holding a heart** that is said to belong to Robert the Bruce who requested that his heart be buried in Jerusalem. King Robert was allied with the Scottish Templars and is honoured at Rosslyn, Europe's "Jerusalem", a site set within lands as sacred as the Holy Land.

The inner pillar capital to the north shows **two swans** – the swan was a very sacred symbol in the Reshel system representing the second manifesting of the sacred bird kingdom and as such carrying high vibrations of the "Solarian" light codes, (the Eagle as a bird of prey is the first and the dove is the third).

On the south capital is a **Green Man (fig 35)** with the vines in the corner of its mouth appearing as if they are fingers commanding "Hush!" This is another indicator that the point is sacred in terms of an initiatory path taken around the chapel. Buehler says that the "Shhhh" breath-sound is the "whispering" through the Unicorn's Horn as a manifesting action according to Maia/Thoth. Buehler has drawn attention to Yeshua's last teaching on the Cross which is all of Ps 22 beginning with "My Father why have you forsaken me." The victory over the Fall begins with "for thou hast heard me from the horns of the unicorns" Ps 22:21. Psalm 92:10 also refers to the horn of the unicorn. In the process of manifestation or transmutation you sound the horn to make a sound. According to Maia/Thoth, in earlier epochs the priests used specific chants to create time portals through the "horn" for the purpose of passing the "seed" of their evolutionary works into the future continuum.

Figure 35: *Green Man whispering "Hush"*

At this point on our journey around the chapel we are indeed reaching the end of the path and a major spiritual victory is in sight.

On the west capital an **alligator** straddles a long-backed beast, and **a piper** in the court of Darius beside a mysterious **unknown (sleeping?) figure** faces east on the capital. In this area we seem to face a conglomerate of energies coming together.

The cross lintel shows **seven virtues and seven vices** on each of its sides though at some time the Gluttony stone in the centre was inter-changed for some reason. It could have been a simple error in replacement when repairs were carried out at some point. John Ritchie in his book Rosslyn Revealed states that Gilbert Haye, the extremely learned tutor to the Sinclair children, has the identical error in his early writings, so it may be that the error was intended from the start. Ritchie believes quite understandably that it was Haye who influenced the design of the lintel.

There is a fantastical animal high on the clerestory wall between the arches in the southeast corner of the nave – it looks like a monkey but its face is not in proportion – it looks rather more like a creature out of our modern fantasy worlds, such as in the film trilogy Lord of the Rings! Such creatures do live in other dimensions, but in our very materialistic world view of recent times it is hard for most people to believe this reality

As we approach the end of the south aisle the carvings seems to reflect the third and final initiation going around the chapel – on the external wall are window niches set on triple layer plinths similar to some of those internally, but nothing unfortunately can be deciphered in the carvings. **There is an X gram** in the window tracery. In the interior, on the window's inner arch we see the **Mexican type of maize (Fig 36).** At the time of the Zeno voyage to Nova Scotia undertaken by William's grandfather in 1398 this maize type was being cultivated in North America–the corn featured in two of the lintels and over the door on the north side, and is now far more mature in size and development. There are **nine mature maize plants (Fig 36)** gracing the archway, the end ones held by angels as they unfold their leaves, and the central one appearing on its end as a trumpet flower. It is harvest time – we started in the northeast in autumn and have progressed round to the southeast to late summer! This journey follows the path of the sun's rising within the year in this northern latitude.

Figure 36: *Mature Maize*

The outer archway encompasses **the twelve disciples**. So the nature (as represented by the maize), the angelic and the human realms are all combined in the window here, for the first time in a rather ostentatious manner. Perhaps the purest or highest order in each kingdom is represented here – the supporting angels, the disciples and the maize are all at the purest level for their kind here. Nine is the number of completion so we can assume the highest devic levels have been accessed and twelve is the number of the Grail, so those who seek have found. Even the **green men and women** at the bases of the arches look equal in age this time, as if to say that all polarities have been balanced, for the green kingdom is but mirroring all other realms at Rosslyn. The focus is often on the elemental realm as that is the place where all rightful connections have to be rekindled with the human realm and beyond. Once the elemental kingdom is healed the rest in effect will follow.

Melchizedech (Fig 37) the highest of priest- kings bears a chalice below the left niche of the window – the chalice is a symbol for the Grail and the receptacle for grace to pour from.

Figure 37: *Mechizedech*

King Darius of Persia asked three apprentices to answer a riddle on the nature of truth, and he favoured Zerubbabel's answer that is featured in its Latin version on the lintel above the steps to the lower chapel. **King Darius** who posed the riddle is carved just to the north end of the lintel bearing the **Latin inscription.** As his reward for answering the riddle correctly, King Darius allowed Zerubbabel to rebuild the ruined temple in Jerusalem, so just as the carvings suggest the culmination of energies are reached and the initiate has progressed well, the theme of Jerusalem returns to haunt us. This is a fine example of how the chapel is multi-levelled and reflects all points of view. The answer to the riddle being "Wine is strong, the king is stronger, women are stronger still but Truth conquers all!" acts as a timely reminder to some of the chapel's main themes – the vine travels around the chapel in and out of the green men's faces; kingship is forever near at hand with reference to Jesus as King of Kings on one of the early lintels and later in the adjacent (south) aisle the Sinclairs as kings of knowledge and wisdom acting as temporal and spiritual advisors to the Scottish kings and vassals of Christ; the women are honoured more in the south aisle that culminates here, and the ancient yet eternal theme of Truth is addressed as follows:

When filled with grace, the initiate is able to utter truth and descend to the lower chapel, where traditionally members of twelve local families met to discuss esoteric affairs.

The chalice that the ancient priest –king Melchizedech bears represents that grace factor, for there is a test presented to the initiates here, beyond which only those who have enough grace can proceed. The dynamic is borne out in the ancient Hebrew translation of the Darius riddle, that describes three states of being that are associated with the grace factor, which the Tree of Life nearby incorporates in its function. When the initiate passes over this threshold she is filled with a state of inner joy and the Christ energy within is carried downstairs to where work of the highest order can commence. It is fitting that the chalice Melchizedech holds faces the spot at which grace occurs – here, according to the state of grace reached, one's inner being has been enlightened three times over, as one walked the south aisle to the top of the steps. The three stages of enlightenment echo the three main stages of initiation undergone in freemasonry. Rosslyn was built on the same philosophical rocks upon which freemasonry unfolded, but Rosslyn is far more. The **wide step** a little down the flight of stairs aligns with the bosses in the Lady Chapel that are on the Rose Line, and allows the pilgrim to assimilate all the energies depicted in the chapel he has walked through. These energies are reflected in the carvings, but the true dynamic quality to them can only be reached inwardly and in utter simplicity / purity of intent, that is found in deep meditation in the lower chapel. The lower chapel indeed dictates this by its nature, for it is the "Christic" half of the Reshel, the female half responsible for all outward manifestation of divine energies being in the upper ground level chapel.

Buehler says that the passage at 1 Esdras 3:10-12 is indicative of the dynamics of what is occurring here – outwardly in this passage the foundations of the temple have been completed and there is much joy, while inwardly the spiritual dynamics are being described.

Further consideration to Melchizedech is fruitful here before passing on. His image is carved in the very last window niche before the steps begin ahead. In Hebrew 6:20 and 7:24 Jesus Christ is seen as a high priest after the order of M. Now we are in the south aisle that is more aligned with the path of the warrior-king whose mantle key members of the Sinclair clan adopted. In Hebrew 4:12-14 there are eight points of "Rest" in four leading to the brilliant logo of God: alive, powerful, beyond the two-mouthed sword. This description of the sword is critical to the Warrior-Priest, and sets up the high priest dynamic which links with the order of Mechizedech. It is interesting that in the Reshel dynamics the two-mouthed sword becomes the silence and implodes, in turn creating duality since the single point / mouth generates two poles – in the chapel at the end of each lintel we see the open mouths of beasts displaying the same principle to create the forms that span the lintels as they implode.

Having gone counter-clockwise around the chapel we have followed the downward spiral in the way that Spirit drops to our level, and we to the lower devic levels. In doing so it is imperative that the intent and right action is pure, as Rosslyn was built to interface humanity with the devic realm, and this is/was no easy task.

The path we have taken also makes a containment field for the northeast heel stone. Appropriately before **St Peter's Altar,** we are in accordance with Peter 2:2-10 in the context of Jesus Christ being the Chief Head Stone. Having recognize the sacred hollowness in the stone, as Peter's name in Hebrew (Kaffa) means, the codes carried by the carvings are fed into it, and the human becomes a priest, in as much the same way that the Sinclair, encoded with the Christic mysteries, becomes the Warrior-Priest. Again, in Matt 24:27-30 the Son of Man as lightening shines from east to west, where the eagles gather over fallen Man (humanity). Man then responds by closing the loop in a west – east direction, just as we have done here. The life of Jesus as Son of Man has been depicted in the north aisle, with his spirit descending from the north east and finally grounding in the north west, whereas the life of Man begins in the southwest, and finally ascends to merge with Christ in the southeast. The two aisles reflect the two-way flow of spirit and humanity, in tandem with the four seasons of nature and their plant forms.

As in St Piat's Chapel in Chartres, the ornamental Apprentice pillar here describes this threshold over which the initiate will pass into other dimensions. It is the portal to the Grail. Buehler refers to the Tree of Knowledge (the Apprentice pillar) as "carrying the mechanical codes for creation via the 8 Shamirs (snakes) that also generate the True Vine that empowers all of Rosslyn and also carries the Devic codes in which the Chapel specializes, in Nature. This Tree of Knowledge is the southeast corner of the Templa Mar format.

Above the stairway lies the final window on the south side, which has **nine cacti with angels** either end holding the cacti by their leaves. Over stairs **a niche in wall** has had some object broken off but still displays a whiskered man with long hair below in relief – this must have been a vital clue as to the history of the development of the ideas held here. There is a Judas dynamic at play within the Reshel here which is beyond the remit of this guide. It does seem possible that the niche held his statue. There was a stone carving of Judas that was of comparable size to fit the niche that was removed from the lower chapel shortly after I had identified it to the chapel staff, and the discovery coincided with the Book of Judas being translated and published. In the book we learn how Judas agreed to betray Jesus in order that his divine plan could be accomplished.

Having circumnavigated the main chapel we have come once again to the Lady Chapel in the east. However, those who know truth are no longer in a linear mode of thinking – they have been released by grace and are worthy to descend past the threshold – carrying the

Christic codes with them to the vault below where the work is of the highest multi-dimensional order. It is there that the inner connections were always made via synergic meditations in small groups; the visions acquired feeding the design of that above.

As we pause on the wide step to integrate the path taken around the chapel, we can look up and see a **"cross pattee" (Fr) (Fig 38)** underneath a boss projecting into the space. The lower chapel stems from a period when the Templars were legitimate in Scotland, and this may be a hidden reference to the fact. There is a local legend that twelve families regularly met here to discuss esoteric affairs…

Figure 38: *Templar Cross under Boss*

Chapter Five:

The Lady Chapel

The east end of Rosslyn Chapel is known as the Lady Chapel. There is always a dance between male and female energies in the chapel, but there is also a state of being that is far less accessible, which lies beyond duality, and which can define the Holy Grail. More and more people are slowly becoming more aware of this deeper reality in their lives. In the Lady Chapel we encounter the densest collection of carvings in the chapel, with angels and green men interfacing one another at the base of several arches, while carvings relating to the human realms adorn the bosses and arches, for the three basic realms of existence (human, angelic and elemental) converge in the Lady Chapel. The female impulse is to be fecund and hence manifest the energies in abundance. This is what can be readily observed in the aptly named Lady Chapel. It lies in the upper storey of the chapel where the female principle is borne out.

At the bases of the **cube-bearing arches, angels** play music on their **various instruments.** They are in effect playing the music of the spheres; a harmony that is of such a high frequency human ears cannot normally hear it. The patterned cubes number 215 if you include one that is blank and two that are broken off – If we add 1 to 215 we reach 216, which was one of the classical numbers for God in the ancient Hebrew tradition, and seen as a triad of 72, which is resonant with the 72 petalled Rose Mystica that Barry Dunford has written an e-zine on. (See Appendix B).

The blank cube (on the north – south line between the Journeyman and "Apprentice" pillars) may represent the silence (in Hebrew the "Selah" factor), that is an essential ingredient in Reshel dynamics. Buehler calls it the +1 factor that is also found in the Reshel rings, where an additional tiny spoke or space lies between a pattern of points regularly spaced on a circle. When I asked Buehler about the number of cubes I counted he remarked "215" in Hebrew would be "Heyeresh" or "Resh-yah" which puts it in the Reshel ball park, connecting Yah (Yahway) with the Chief Head Stone".

Above the Lady Chapel point the most magnificently carved pinnacles thrust heavenward. They more than likely represent the heavenly energies of the Ennead. (Interestingly there were nine original knights in the Knights Templar order!) According to Maia/Thoth, in an ancient mystery school there was a conscious group of initiates contacting a body of angelic energies known as the Ennead within the Seraphim realm. The group consisted of five men and four women, and this ritual was known as the Elisaphane Exchange. The pinnacles fit this pattern of four and five, and we will look at them after describing the rest of the Lady Chapel below.

There is also one pillar to discuss that links in with the Lady Chapel and is beyond its boundaries:

The Mari Pillar and the Templa Mar

The Mari pillar is on the central axis and set above the central altar in the chapel. There may well have been a Black Madonna on the pillar here when it was in its first stage as a chapel from 1480- 1585 approximately, since other Catholic cathedrals in France and Spain that still possess such Figures share the same Reshel geometry that is present in Rosslyn, and such buildings were designed under Templar influence e.g. Chartres in France and Montserrat in Spain. The Mari pillar generates an eight pointed wheel that spins in the etheric and emanates very high spiritual light codes. The inner Templars worked with the eight pointed wheel and to a large degree it was their main spiritual mechanism.

Rosslyn is physically oriented to the east although its etheric orientation within the Templa Mar format orientates it north, and the layout of the pillars grounds this orientation in the physical realm also. Specialist meditation groups working with the Reshel process find that the directions align thus too. In terms of the qualities assigned to the eight directions, there is a close correlation between Amerindian and

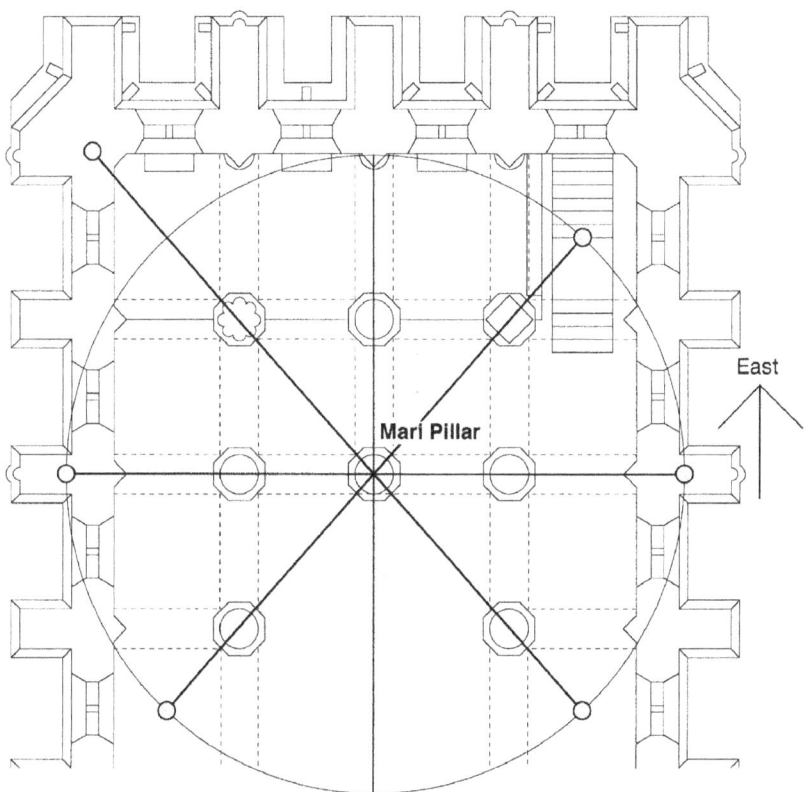

Eight Pole rings around Mari pillar and Templar Cross

early Celtic systems indicating that they are similar in quality and nature – this is because The Templa Mar format is designed specifically for those groups and temples that are working for the purposes of assisting Earths transition into the Metatronic realm. Other cultures and tribes in various places and times may have other cardinal directional codes, but Rosslyn displays the Templa Mar format in very exact forms. The gate to the higher angelic realms is in the north, whereas the devic or elemental heavens are in the south. In terms of spiritual dynamics, William Buehler describes the Templa Mar as a "time continuum reality frame", which is created by thought forms and supported by relevant energy systems. He regards the Templa

Mar as the most efficient format used in temples across time both to restore the fallen Continuum and to achieve the spiritual objectives presented by its creation. Overleaf is a diagram of how the Templa Mar is marked by the layout of the pillars in Rosslyn Chapel, the eight pole rings around the Mari pillar generating the ancient and sacred Templa Mar cross:

There is only one reality in non-linear time (perceived by us as the Metatronic reality) but it is convenient for consciousness to work on projects in the three continua of past, present and future.

According to Bill Buehler **the central Mari pillar** is the Vau (6) pole within the geometry, and is drawn as a circle or sphere with a line descending from it as seen in the main window tracery above the pillar.

As we face the main centre altar there are three pillars beyond that demarcate the west border of the Lady Chapel. They are best viewed from outside the Lady Chapel (stand behind the main altar and look east toward the Lady Chapel), so you can see the row of pillars forming the west edge of the Lady Chapel.

The Three Pillars of Wisdom

The names for these pillars vary according to Masonic and other traditions. In Masonic terms the central one is called the **Journeyman Pillar** and this lies behind the **Mari pillar**, the one to its left is the **Master pillar,** while the one to the right is commonly known as the **Apprentice Pillar.** Looking at these three pillars we can also view them as the three degrees of initiation, but a cautionary note here: things always flow two ways so it is rather easy to label them in a linear fashion and view them too simplistically when in reality we are dealing here with states of mind where everything is in a dynamic state. Later we will look at the interdependent and more intricate roles the pillars play.

The Journeyman's Pillar

Directly behind the Mari pillar is the Journeyman's pillar, which is very important in the Kabbalah tradition. Unlike its neighbours to either side that are more richly carved, it nevertheless performs functions on more than one level – on a higher level it is known in Reshel terms as the Layooesh that bridges Heaven with Earth in a pillar or tube of light, the inner pillar known as the Zoi pillar. It is the vehicle for our ascent into Heaven in a non-physical sense.

The Journeyman has a most **unusual Green Man (Fig 39)** on its capital, facing northwest. It is very like a coral charm that the gypsies used and is now in the collection held by the archivist for the Knights Templar branch of masons local to Rosslyn. The coral is known as Brainstone coral because its patterning is similar to the DNA patterning, and at the time it was on display the charm bore a strong likeness to the carving in the chapel, so much so that I now call the carving the Green Coral rather than a Green Man.

Figure 39: *The Green Coral /Skull*

It is appropriate to see it here as the Layooesh Pillar works with substances down to a microcosmic levels, and therefore affects the very DNA of our substance – our DNA will be radically altered by subtle spiritual forces when we ascend, and this has been a subject in recent years among some thinkers in the New Age movement who focus on more refined / advanced aspects of life.

The Master Pillar

The Master pillar is designed in straight lines and this is the equivalent to the male pole when taking the three pillars as a whole. Buehler writes that in Solomon's Temple the Master Mason's Pillar was seen as Boaz and is the male Heel Stone that processes and then feeds spiritual seed-codes into the system while the Apprentice pillar (Yahchen) acts like a female generator that provides the mechanisms for processing the seed codes it has received from Boaz. This is why in the southeast we see many references to flowering and abundance in nature, essentially a female role.

The **dancing Green Man** known as Jack in the Green **(see back cover)** is on the north face of the lintel leading from the Boaz pillar on front of the Lady Chapel. An early reference to a Green Man figure lies in the holy book the Qur'an where he was known as Al-Khidir, whom Moses tests three times and who eventually proves himself to be good, although his replies appear ambiguous at first. The placement of Jack in the Green here seems almost humorous, because he is on the threshold of a lintel facing a route to the top of the stairway where a test or riddle is written, and this in turn marks the spot where man is tested. (One of my favourite moments conducting tours was when an internationally acclaimed Morris dancer sang a wonderful rendition of the English folk song Jack in the Green downstairs in the crypt on May Day!)

The Apprentice Pillar

Much has been already written about this pillar – it has been seen as the Tree of Knowledge that tempted Eve and Adam. Its Norse name is Yggdrasil , a tree guarded by serpents at the centre of the world and connected with the underworld. The same pillar is Joachim / Yah-Chen in Solomon's temple in Masonic/Reshel circles respectively. **The eight serpents (Fig 40)** are connected to the Hebrew Letter Nun and its appropriate dynamics here – without going into detail here we can think of them as holding the life force (Hindu: Kundalini), so much so that we see them spewing the greenery from their mouths and sending it up to the top of the pillar where it goes hence in all directions around the chapel.

If the pillar is considered to hold the secrets of Creation, the chapel's Reshel geometry defines the spot. The pillar is an important geometric node that represents a portal into the higher worlds that are accessed below in the Lower Chapel.

Figure 40: *The serpents of Yggdrasil*

The pillar has become the modern day symbol for Rosslyn Chapel due to the fantastic story of the apprentice murder at Rosslyn. As we discussed earlier, this is nothing more than a myth to align Rosslyn further with the ancient craft of masons that stemmed from Solomon's times when their architect Hiram Abif the architect was murdered. The initiations in the upper chapel undertaken may well have been performed from ancient times, so the carving of Hiram Abif as an old sacrificial hero is not out of place. Like the corn god who was sacrificed in nature-worshipping cultures, cultural figures arose in the human arena too. However, since the time of Christ the old sacrificial ways are no longer so relevant–they make way instead for the White path that does not depend on sacrifice but rather depends on a factor of grace. The current transition offers much confusion, as the well-worn Red Path and the incoming White path often collide in worldly affairs. Both are still relevant but in the future only the new one will prevail. A purer meaning to the Apprentice pillar would sidestep the issue of the alleged murder and focus on the element of grace required in the Ascension process.

The Four Altars along the East Wall

There are four sub-altars along the east wall constitute a retro chapel within the overall chapel, and were allegedly dismantled after the Reformation due to the new religious laws and subsequently restored by the Victorians. When the Victorians restored Rosslyn as an active church they carried out a lot of renovation on the carvings in the Lady Chapel, and yet the detail of their restoration work fits in marvellously with the overall intent of the chapel. For instance, the **angels in the window arches** are all from that period – some of them wear feathers as if they were birds, and the birds were seen as Solarian creatures (beasts carrying codes from the central sun in the universe). It could be that the Victorians accurately restored previous stonework, or they could have created new stone designs that seem in keeping with the original intent of the whole work.

St Matthew's Altar

The sub-altar in the northeast of this beautiful chapel is called St Matthew's, the alternative ecclesiastical name for the whole chapel also. The Collegiate Chapel we see today is the second version of St Matthew's – there was one by that name built in the eleventh century in what is now the lower cemetery created during the Victorian period when a need for a parish cemetery arose.

The dedication to St Matthew is important–St Matthew's feast day is the autumn equinox, a time of the year considered auspicious for spiritual development in Druid times, and also in other spiritual traditions such as Hinduism. The days are growing darker from this point until the winter solstice, and there is a reawakening of one's inner forces (and the earth's inner forces too, according to Steiner). Reinforcing the idea of spiritual renewal, there is a crack in the clerestory east wall that allows a light to shine through onto the **west wall** opposite on St Matthew's Day – this wall was a bare wall once but altered by the Victorians to make way for an organ gallery. It puzzled the writers of early guides to the chapel as to why there was a blank wall on the chapel – but the notion of light of the vernal equinox falling on the back wall once a year is not new – some of the ancient cairns of the Beaker folk in the Bronze Age were designed with the same dynamic at play. At such sites in Ireland and Scotland, I have dowsed that these sites, like Rosslyn, are attuned to the "Metatronic" frequencies. St Matthew's Day is also the time of Michaelmas, when the quality of the archangel Michael draws close to us all and our inner fire quickens. The setting of St Matthew's Altar in the northeast corner of the church is important for cosmological ideas also. The Templars regarded the northeast to be of particular significance because the redemptive powers of the spirit entered the earth here. Michael the angelic archetype of redemption is appropriately linked with St Matthew's altar here – his feast day is close by on September 29th and his own mission as a dragon slayer was to redeem mankind. (**Archangel Michael** is featured in the huge single Victorian stained glass window on the south clerestory, and in the south end section of the roof carvings.)

Astronomical Alignments

Research from various sources indicates that this time of year is astronomically potent during the time of the chapel's dedication on St Matthew's Day. Independent researcher Jeff Nisbet of New Jersey says that if you look at the Starchart of September 21st, 1450, which he believes to be Rosslyn's date, eight heavenly bodies were visible in a narrow area of sky. The resonant of the constellation Virgo and its two, Zaniah and Porimma, are explained in his article. **See Appendix D**

Even more astonishingly, Rab Wilkie who lives in Canada has discovered resonant and significant rare Grail constellations occurred on the dawn horizon on both the consecration date September 11th 1446 and in 2008. **See Appendix D**

The boss (Fig 41) projecting down on front of St Matthew's altar used to house a beehive entrance / exit from which bees would occasionally emerge. Their stone beehive was usually entered from outside via a rose in the small tower above this area. These sacred creatures were believed to possess special powers and so for them to emerge here in the northeast where the core spiritual impulse is borne is also very apt. Most unfortunately all the bees were killed when the hive was fumigated in order to protect the visitors from possible accidents – the netting can still be seen over the boss!

There are many other signs to observe in the northeast: The external

Figure 41: *Bee Entrance*

arches in the window above St Matthew's altar show **a person clutching his ear** on the left inner arch as if to say "Hear no evil" – or is it a covert reference to the celestial music within the Lady Chapel? **A dove descends (Fig 42)** at the end of the left outer arch, while a peacock struts out its feathers on the end of the right outer one. The peacock too was generally regarded as sacred by the Templars. The stone peacock may be a whooper swan. Both the dove and the swan were regarded as "Solarian" birds by the inner Templars who created these symbols to indicate that the high solar codes of the Metatronic full light spectrum were present. The descending dove brings the spiritual energies down to earth in order that the earth can be redeemed. Apparently our present cycle is the one inducing the main Fall Factor so an additional emphasis is now put into that large effort in Redemption (Maia/Thoth).

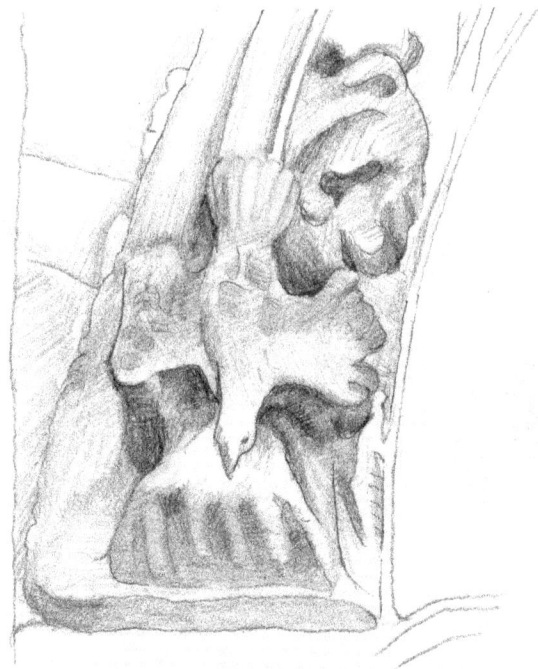

Figure 42: *Dove Descending*

On the inner right external arch is a **Green Man with webbed feet**. The Figures with webbed feet or scaly lower halves to their bodies are reminiscent of Lemurian times (pre-Atlantean) and since the northeast seems to indicate the beginning of the journey round the chapel that was described earlier, it seems appropriate to place a very early form of Green Man here. There is also a buttress in the northeast corner, just before rounding the corner, where **a Figure with a Puck-like face and webbed feet** stands. It is interesting that the **angels' hair** is often shaped into **a crescent around their heads.** The crescent was an early symbol like a "pre-form" used to set up a creation field, and in the period Rosslyn was built, local eminent family crests bore that sign. The interior arch of St Matthew's Window is no exception to the Rosslyn norm of bearing succulent flowers that are sevenfold. The female creation number in its most complete form is seven, and flowers are attributed to the female. The nature kingdom in abundance is honoured in the northeast window. All realms are honoured within

Figure 43: *Wild Green Man*

the Lady Chapel. The realms of the human, angelic, high archangelic and devic (nature beings) all converge here. The human for example is represented by the **Dance of Death** on the diagonal ribs on the ceiling above St Matthew's Altar where nine courtiers and seven commoners are arranged. It serves as a reminder that in the higher planes, all people are equal, regardless of their earthly roles.

St Mary's Altar

On the exterior arch of the window a very **wild Green Man (Fig 43)** baring his teeth is at the base of the arch on the left. Since the female energies are closely affined with the path of nature wisdom, it is fitting that the window associated with the only female saint along the east wall bears a particularly powerful looking Green Man.

The outer right arch shows a **pelican**, which was the symbol for the Stewarts. Their ancestors were the Merovingian kings in France who are linked with both the story of Mary Magdalene's exodus to France and also the path of ancient earth wisdom guarded by the female initiates. The theme of abundant nature is exemplified in the **two angels** at the end of the window arch whose heads are piled high with greenery.

The interior of the window shows angels around the niches as usual – **the left niche angel** has an equal-armed cross on her head and holds victorious palm fronds in a cross shape. The "X-gram", as Buehler names this cross shape, is close to the central "green" axis that extends into the glen from the chapel. Fecundity is illustrated too by **the Star of Bethlehem** on the first vertical boss in the ceiling that shows the birth of Christ with the Madonna and child facing south (the south was the direction associated most with the female creative energies in the eightfold wheel tradition).

On the east wall, we see **King Robert the Bruce's death mask** above a capital to the left of St Mary's window. This is one of many links that Rosslyn makes with Jerusalem. Robert the Bruce wished that his heart would be buried in Jerusalem, and the mission failed. The wish is honoured more than a century on by portraying his death mask in a building that reputedly bears the same layout as the foundations of the ruined Solomon's temple in Jerusalem. That building is Rosslyn, and the land around it is holy.

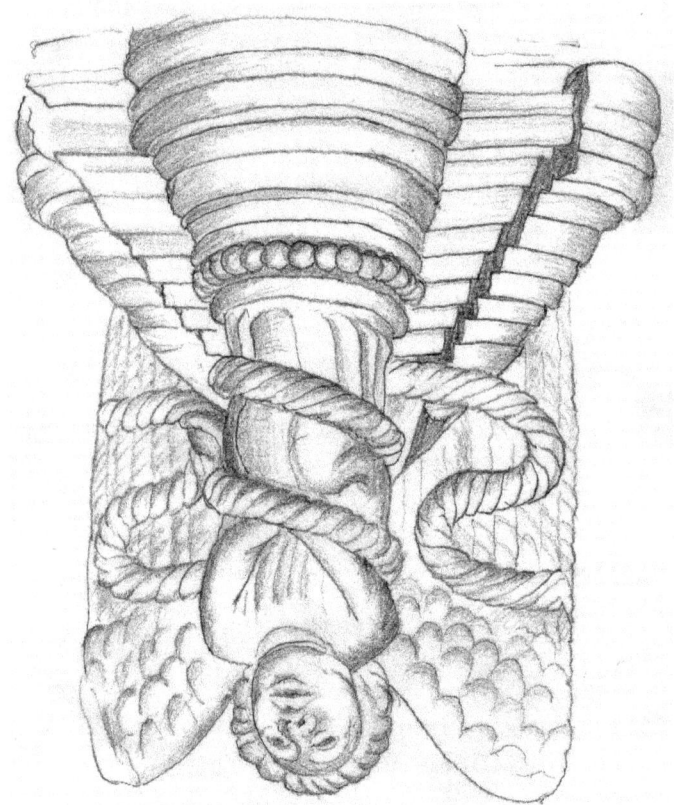

Figure 44: *Shemyazza*

Below Bruce under a niche lies **an inverted angel (Fig 44),** with ropes around him. This hanging angel is often perceived as Lucifer, but there is also an older story from Babylonian and Hebrew mythology that tells of Shemyazza, a high archangel whose body of angels were sent to earth to assist mankind. They had strict instructions not to interfere in the physical realms but some of them fornicated with the female folk, and so Shemyazza shouldered the responsibility for the breaking of that promise with God. He was cast out of Heaven until such time as mankind had understood enough to live wisely, and rectify the error they and the angels had committed. This version of the tale of Shemyazza hints strongly that humans are responsible even for the fate of the angels, and that there will come a time when the fallen angel can be returned to his high position. Another interpretation of Shemyazza concerns a tale that he knows the explicit name of God and has made a deal with a human Ishthar to tell her the name. Since he is carved in the Lady Chapel, below the cubes that may bear the hidden codes for his name, this tale is intriguing.

Figure 45: *Aleph Symbol*

Humans have free choice, and affect the beings in the other realms that are not so free, like the angels and devas/nature spirits who are seen here in the cross arches, the angels playing the music of the spheres and the green men supporting them. We all in fact support each other in the journey toward the light. Often the symbols cross boundaries as we know them in our linear world – on the east wall many of the angels appear to be clad in feathers as mentioned earlier. The feathered creatures are generally the birds, and the bird kingdom is sacred to the Reshel, as they are aligned with the Metatronic realm where a central sun of all suns resides, called Mazuriel. It seems appropriate that on the east wall, aligned with the Rose Line, the feathered angels would be helping create a spiritual connection with the realm of Metatron.

Between St Mary's and St Andrew's altars there is a miniature temple on the wall at the side of a column. Under its right hand projection there is **a simple motif (Figure 45)** that is replicated in the same position under all temple projections beside each altar on the east wall, apart from the final one, St Peter's Altar, which is above the stairs. The motif appears there is under the left hand projection instead so it can still be viewed easily from the Lady Chapel.

It resembles an open tulip with the side petals shaped into long horns – this is a classic version of the Aleph or creation field being set up (the crescent shape is another example), that is largely concerned with creation dynamics. It can also be seen as a bull's head with long horns – and God was perceived as its unseen rider. It is as though these templates feed into the Rose Line and carry the codes of new creation. If Rosslyn is a New Jerusalem, the intent to build Heaven on Earth is fed into all the Rose Line along the altar line here. Since the principle of creation applies to all realms simultaneously, all realms are represented in the Lady Chapel here, as the chief creation codes are all contained in this area and spread a long distance here via the chief ley, the Rose Line.

Before we arrive at St Andrew's Altar we cross the central axis of the chapel that intersects with the Rose Line. This is the Ulta or Glory point in the Reshel geometry. The Reshel geometry provides an etheric blueprint for the chapel that boosts its frequencies to the point where very high (Metatronic) energies reside – according to Maia/Thoth the Solarian races reside there in the central sun of the universe.

The Ulta point in the Reshel is the portal that allows access to this realm in the Metatronic light spectrum, and was too holy to work with directly – other "trigger" points in the chapel were used instead.

St Andrew's Altar

This altar lies below the next window. Outside, **Mercury** is carved on a low lying buttress between St Peter's and St Andrew's window. He faces over the lower chapel and down the glen, and by his position seems to create a link between the two levels of the chapel. While Pan is appropriately situated on external wall on the central axis on the Reshel's "Horizon of Thoth" that keys into nature, Mercury is on the adjacent buttress and likewise is looking east to the horizon – where on St Matthew's Day 1446 he appeared on the horizon at dawn. (see Appendix D). In 2008 he reappeared in this rare rising, and the timely dawn appearance heralds in a new consciousness associated with Ascension to those who, like the Magi of old, are studying the charts esoterically.

Figure 46: *Green Musician*

There are a range of diverse worn **bird carvings** on the external window arches. Birds like Mercury are associated with the element of air. Furthermore **a curious Figure (Fig 46)** is playing what appears to be a "green" instrument high in the left arch, the plant tendrils becoming its air pipes. Could it be that each of the altars is affiliated with one of the four main elements?

Inside the window arch we see **twelve flowers,** with a **thirteenth one in the centre**. There is a widespread esoteric belief that we are on the edge of a new era, and that there will be a new and additional thirteenth zodiacal sign born to herald in the new era – this will be the energy of the Dolphin/cetacean or Unicorn. The thirteen plants could refer to the number thirteen, which we have referred to previously in terms of its association with a new and vital continuum.

Under the right hand niche **seven horns encircle an angel** holding a garland. She has a cross in the centre of her crown area along with **crescent-shaped hair.** There are several angels with hair shaped into crescents – the crescent is another representation of Aleph the letter for Creation – so these are angels who bear the codes for Creation or new paradigms in consciousness, much in the same way as Moses and St Margaret do. The repetition of the sevenfold theme above the angel suggests perfection in the Female pole of Creation, since seven represents the perfected female form. The entire Lady Chapel can be seen as the Vault of Creation.

St Peter's Altar

This altar is above the steps that lead to the lower chapel Peter is Kaffa in Hebrew, meaning Hollow stone. The altar was always left bare and unadorned, in the custom of the hollow or void on which all of nature depends. The void is literally below the altar. The final altar is also associated with the equivalent Celtic symbol: the Cauldron of Creation. Kaffa as a letter sets up a creation field in the Reshel light codes as deciphered by Buehler. It is from the hollow stone that substance is created.

Fig 47: *Green man above St Peter's Altar*

There are **nine curly kales** in the window arc meeting at the centre with a cardinal cross. Curly kale was revered by Templars – it is linked with the forces of regeneration, the main theme of the chapel in many respects. Nine being Completion, it suggests that regeneration is complete, in this area fed by the void below. The altar is bordered by a window arch whose ends depict two green men–**the plants divide into two in a pile on the head** of the one on the left. The division of one whole part into two parts seems to signify an essential first stage in the creation process. The two green men at either end create a "dipole". On the opposite side to the Green Man shown in the diagram **the Green Man** on the right hand side or pole is crowned and piled with greenery. He is **poking out his tongue** – perhaps a gesture or greeting encountered by Prince Henry Sinclair on his voyage to Nova Scotia. In mythology, when elementals, guardians, devas or deities were invited as honoured guests to ritual events they were offered nourishment including beverages, and they came, their tongues rolled "like straws" to drink / sick up. This suggestion by Rab Wilkie is one of many lingual possibilities. The overall carving of the two green men here seems to suggest that the first Green Man on the left is at the start of an energy flow, indicated by the process of division into smaller units, while the second Green Man on the right is receiving the fruits of the energy flow. This bipolar dynamic is often shown in the chapel in small areas that do not normally draw attention.

On the left bottom arch of the window is **an angel wearing a jewel** in the centre of his brow (classical third eye point in esoteric physiology systems).

Being above the stairway, **St Peter's Altar (Fig 47)** overlooks the position where an L-shaped turn takes place in the Lady Chapel, where we turn from the horizontal north-south plane above to the vertical plane at right angles to this, leading down to the lower chapel. The L shape signals incoming new dimensions that can only be accessed through the third eye or other senses. Along with many of the geometric patterns and dynamics, the all important L shift is explained far more fully in *The Spiritual Purpose to Rosslyn*.

The stone tracery in the window forms **an X** as in other key sites in the chapel. As mentioned earlier, the X gram is a symbol for a multi-dimensional portal. Angels with X grams on their heads grace the each end of the window arch outside. Inside, at the bottom of the window arch is an angel crossing scythes into an **X gram**. A similar figure appears in the opposite end of the Lady Chapel on the exterior of the first window on the north side. The two wide human faces mentioned in our walk around the chapel face each other in opposite corners of the Lady Chapel - here above St Peter's Altar **the face (Fig 48)** looks content and enlightened, in contrast to the startled one in the opposite corner where our journey began! The content looking face appears to seal the journey described around the chapel.

This pair of wide faces is unique and appears at only the start and the end of a journey around the aisles of the chapel.

Figure 48: *Face of Satisfaction (compare with Fig 4: Face of Awakening)*

The ceiling arches are very ornate in this southeast corner. On the south-facing rib above the stair, leading from the southeast corner across to the northwest side are four Figures: **a warrior with sword and spear, a monk drinking, death and a man.** On the north-facing rib are a further four Figures – a **queen, a lady seated, a lady praying, and a warrior**. Could the lady be Queen Margaret who was so fond of the Culdees, an enigmatic Christian group who bridged the old Druid ways with the new Christian religion? This may be why the Sinclairs regarded the queen highly as one of their patron saints; many of the plant carvings in the chapel would have their roots in the Celtic knowledge of healing plants, an area in which the Culdees were adepts. It is more than likely that many of the families the Sinclairs connected with when they first settled in this area were originally Celtic, rather than Norman settlers like themselves. Perhaps these families held long healing traditions that used a deep knowledge of the plant kingdom. It is said that many families in Scotland were able to retain their lands and were given feudal privileges as they won the trust of their new lords of the Norman invasion. For example, the Abernethy family of Hawthornden during the early period of Rosslyn lived at Hawthornden Castle a mile of so upstream from Rosslyn... These landowners would have had links with the local Cistercian abbey of Newbotyl (now Newbattle Abbey) and also by default the Templars at Balantradoch. All of the sites were well connected by tracks long disappeared off the landscape, but discernable on old maps. Jeff Nisbet believes the Abernethys of Hawthornden were originally from Ireland – there is no telling how long ago they moved to Hawthornden – they may well have been connected to the ancient Culdee headquarters of Abernethy in Fife, which in turn held semi-mythical connections to Bride of Ireland. At Hawthornden there is evidence that a hermit dwelled in caves hewn into the sandstone cliffs. The hermetic tradition was typical of the later Celtic period. If indeed the Abernethies did carry their Culdee connections with them, family members may well have been present in ceremonies in the lower chapel before Rosslyn was built – an oral tradition says local families frequented the room for esoteric purposes.

The queen on this diagonal arch may not be anyone in particular in these carvings, but could be the representation in the human realm of that which the retro-chapel is named after–the Lady/Shekinah/ Divine Feminine.

A clue to the higher harmonies that are focussed on at the east end lies in what is sculptured above the Lady Chapel. There we find nine pinnacles of great beauty bordering the outer edges of the rectangular Lady Chapel. These pinnacles are reaching. skywards to the angelic realms. The number nine is associated with completion and high wisdom, and includes in its number both male and female qualities.

Chapter Six:

The Nine Pinnacles above the Lady Chapel and Ceiling

The exterior pinnacles bear witness to the very high angelic realms to which the Lady Chapel is dedicated, as their design and layout represent the nine energies of the Ennead within the Seraphim, an archangelic order who have among their objectives the resurrection of this Universe, which has been Earth's objective ever since the mythical Fall. The names of the various Archai are listed in **Appendix C.** The Ennead was invoked in an ancient mystery school ritual involving an Elisa priesthood of four women and five men who were in harmony with the nine members of the archangel Ennead. Their sacred ritual was known as an Elisaphane Exchange according to Maia/Thoth.

There is a rich layering of interpretation for the carvings in the chapel, and one of the relevant layers is the Celtic. According to Fionntulach of the Order of Culdees a hermetic order with an unbroken lineage from early times, the Celts would know the nine pinnacles as the nine fold ones, or the Awakened Ones of Celtic mythology, being sacred receivers of divine light. These nine receivers are duplicated in the ancient ritual described above. The light was both received and returned, for in all spiritual dynamics there is a two-way flow / exchange of energies.

The Five Pinnacles

The set of five pinnacles along the eastern extremity follow a north-south axis. Five is essentially the male number that acts as a seeding mechanism as earlier discussed. Lying in a straight line along the edge of the Lady Chapel's roof they are seeding the Rose Line with high cosmic energies. Three of these five pinnacles are pyramid – shaped and as we shall see later they act as special posts within the overall design. The first pyramid is set in the northeast and its position is a key one as we shall see later.

The Four Pinnacles

The polarities of the female and male are balanced here as elsewhere in the chapel.

The number four is the female energy of multiple gestation, fecundity and manifestation.

Energetically there is a set of four remaining pinnacles that make a rectangle or basic creation vault, below which the rich carvings of the Lady Chapel lie. The four female forms are represented by two pairs of double pinnacles on the north and south sides. (Observers have remarked that even the shapes of the pinnacles are more graceful and curvy!). The bases of each pair of female pinnacles consist of an octagon and a hexagon, and the patterns of the first pair on the north side are similar to their counterpart pair on the facing south side The hexagon and octagon set up a dynamic known as the "pillar and heap", or in Reshel terminology they become the connective and form The hexagon can be portrayed as the dweller of divine fire, and the octagon is seen as the manifested form resulting from the fire codes.

The first female pinnacle bears an octagonal base that denotes a giver of form, and we see a myriad of forms below in the Lady Chapel here. The second female pinnacle on the north side is hexagonal in form with five hollow projections rather like giant candleholders moulded in stone below the base. Interestingly, the sixth one is concealed beneath the base at the east end – so we have a 5 + 1 pattern. As with the cubes in the Lady Chapel, a given number + 1 is worth noting, as the extra one denotes the higher creation principle borne by the Hebrew concept of the Selah or Unmanifest God that lies behind that which is manifested. Similarly in the Celtic tradition there are five normal senses and then a sixth hidden one that brings everything into focus and awareness by bringing in the spiritual light to all the previous senses. This is the dynamic that seems to be at play here. The hexagon is seen as the pillar in the temple, the bridging mechanism, or the grace factor at play. It represents one of the three states required in Creation. These three states are constantly interweaving in hundreds of systems in the chapel: the seed, the connective and the manifestation.

The Northeast Pyramid

The next pinnacle is the first one in a line of five that crown the east wall, and it lies in the northeast, where the redemptive power of spirit flows into the earth. This is akin to the serpent or worm boring through the centre of the stone. In early Christian traditions Christ was seen as the serpent or dragon that brought healing and regeneration. In the Reshel the serpent is called the Shamir and it relates to alchemical manifestation. By its very nature it is related to temple building, and so traditionally the cornerstone was placed in the northeast in any Templar edifice.

> *The stone which the builders eliminated is become*
> *the headstone of the corner*
> Psalms 118:18–23 particularly v 22:

Here in the northeast we find the first pinnacle shaped like a pyramid a powerful and ancient symbol. It is decorated on two of its faces with twenty one inverted hearts in its top section and twelve hearts in each of the other two vertical sections.

On a thin sliver of the pyramid pointing due eastwards are eight hearts in their normal upright position. It is as though the inverted hearts belong to a higher dimension and these eight represent the earthly arena where things are more fixed, and may refer to systems of eight such as our human chakras or musical octaves. The angelic flow of love is displayed in the downward pointing hearts while the upward pointing hearts represent the human flow of love. It can be epitomised in the following New Testament passage:

> We know that we have passed from death unto life, because we love the Brethren.
> He that loveth not his brother abideth in death.
> Whosoever hateth his brother is a murderer: and ye know that no murderer hath eternal life abiding in him.
> 1 John: 3:14–15

I call it the two-way flow between the lower and higher heart, bearing in mind that the higher heart resides in what is called the Eden Point within the Reshel. In the human body a point in harmony with the Eden point is set at the centre top of the ribcage, with the Eden Point at the base of the sternum.

The chapel can be seen as the Garden of Eden set in stone, with its cornerstone in the northeast aligning with the Eden point. On the second of the two decorated sides there is another decorated heart in the centre. It faces southeast, which esoterically was seen as the Path of the Mother. The heart could represent the planet Venus, which makes a heart-shape when orbiting the Earth. Here we have the male and female held in a state of independence and balance, as the foremost male seed (represented by the first in line of the five aligned male pinnacles) contains within its structure the essence of the female as symbolized by the triple seven. This is a universal truth in that all male functions bear an essential female inward function and vice versa, so we may see these 21 hearts as the essence of this stone here. Returning to the pyramid, the twelve hearts in each of the two lower sections may reflect the Grail archetype in an As Above, So Below principle. The vertical sections are drawn in proportion of 2:2:3 which add up to the sacred number 7 when taken as a whole.

Inversion of Symbols

When any Figure or sign is inverted one must take note – the eye usually sees an object first in its inverted position, and then fixes it in an upright position, but it is also possible in a higher state of mind to see into the dynamics of vision and behold the object before it is in a fixed position for the normal intellect to deal with. In spiritual dynamics there is a principle at work called the Flashing Universe Dynamics, where things are not fixed but fluid and continually flashing between inverted and upright positions, or rapidly reversing polarities.

For instance, when one who can tune into extremely high frequencies will sense the energy flowing in a particular direction, someone in a more mundane / linear reality will sense the energy as flowing in the opposite direction. In sites with Metatronic frequencies the flow of energy will be going in both directions – and so an inverted symbol at Rosslyn belies the high frequencies it is portraying.

Midway along the north side lays the next pyramidal pinnacle, on the central axis. There is a tiny sliver of six plants in their upright position contrasting with the inverted remainder on the stone, much in the same manner that the hearts do in the northeast pinnacle. The six here seems to connect energetically with the central window opposite with its Vau or 6 vibration / letter. In the southeast the seventh pinnacle is the final pyramid in the male group of pinnacles and exhibits five petalled flowers in twelve divisions on two sides, repeating the theme of doubling the 12 seen at the other end of the line in the northeast pinnacle. These three pyramids give the distinct impression that they are acting as sentinels or knights in stone, and would link in well with the trinity of command posts for the Ennead mentioned earlier. The five petalled flowers numerically increase in each of the three vertical sections, starting with only 2, then 4 and finally 6 in the top section. The configuration suggests a Spirit to Matter flow. We are reminded that while the Lady Chapel, with its strong links to nature, is offered up to the highest possibilities in the Divine Plan for the Earth, the chapel is also grounding the light. In other words, there is always a two-way flow of energy between Earth and Cosmos or Sky, and the pinnacles act as transmitters for the exchange.

The eighth (hexagonal) pinnacle around the corner on the south side belongs to the remaining female pair. The pattern here is very elaborate as each flower is set within a triangle. With regard to the different functions of basic numbers, the 3 or 6 is a connective between the embryonic stage (5 or 10/1) and its fruit (4 or 8) – this pinnacle may be concerned with making connections between the seeding line of five and the extreme pinnacles in the north and south that are concerned with manifesting or creating new life forms that are in perfect harmony with one another.

Figure 49: *Three Green Women*

The last female pinnacle on the south side is the ninth pinnacle in the cycle, and is adorned with five female green women – faces surrounded by foliage (note that unlike the green men who sprout vegetation from their facial orifices, the green women are never defaced in such a manner). These faces are unique and like the flowers on the

114 • *The Spiritual Meaning of Rosslyn's Carvings*

adjacent pillar **a set of three green women (Fig 49)** decrease in size as one descends signifying a Spirit to Matter flow of energy. They seem to portray the triple goddess, and then on a lower part of the adjacent facet there are a further two faces of equal rather than diminishing size. The faces total five, a classically male number so the sequence seems to set up a dynamic where the female and male energies interchange. Moreover the base, although subtly still octagonal, is almost rounded or one-sided. One and five both signify the male seed energy, so perhaps the cycle is renewed as the female images "become" via the form a new male seed, so creating a new level in the angelic realms to which these pinnacles reach. It is like an endless spiralling of energies that perpetuate a cycle of exchange between the lower and upper planes of existence. Perhaps this final pinnacle in the south is round rather than many- sided like its companions because perfection is seen as eternal and a round shape best reflects that idea of never-ending.

These beautiful pinnacles were, after all, built at a high level at which normally man could not feast their eyes on them. We can only view them due to the temporary gantry erected. Such elaborately carved pinnacles appear to be dedicated to the rarefied realms of higher angels.

The three goddesses face southeast, on the axis known as the Path of the Mother. The Templars worked with the eightfold wheel that embraced eight directions. In terms of the ley lines in Europe, the Path of the Mother pointed southeast, from Sligo Bay in the west of Ireland to Mount Sinai in Egypt. Catherine of Sinai was one of the patron saints of the Sinclairs. Could this be her face we see here in triplicate? A delicate beading above the female faces suggests a sacred thread or connection to the divine.

The Ceiling

Returning inside, the ceiling is a beautiful barrel-vaulted shape that resembles an upturned ship. Fittingly the ship was a symbol for the soul in ancient cultures. The carvings are a magnificent piece of craftwork, set in a pattern of squares that are festooned with flowers in the first four sections and stars in the final section. The glories of nature and skies combine in the roof design. The final star clad section appears to encode the chapel's destiny as a Metatronic temple which serves the All.

There have been many theories about what the ceiling means, but it was added by William Sinclair's offspring, who as owner of the castle when his father died also built the dowager house in the forest for his mother to live in. His landscaping programme undertaken around the chapel in the early sixteenth century shows a strong appreciation and love of nature.

The ceiling displays a love of flowers likewise, and if you mathematically even out the distribution of squares so each square is equal in size, an inverted cross of Lorraine is displayed. This may have been a subtle or hidden reflection of the Sinclair's support of the Stewarts at the time, as according to J. Nisbet **(see Appendix D)** the Stewarts descended from the House of Lorraine with its Merovingian dynastic roots of which so many have written speculatively.

The fact that the cross is inverted is also quite significant, as it draws further attention to its meaning, as do the other carvings in the chapel that are inverted. Following on from the sections with lilies, daisies, roses and multiflori, the As Above So Below principle is borne out in the final section replete with stars. There used to be a solitary hand raised in the northern half at the bottom right corner. This in Hebrew lettering was the Yud, the open hand, and is in the correct position if a Reshel pattern is inherent in the roof section of stars. (The Yud is placed in the bottom right corner of a basic triangle concerned with elevating Matter into Spirit.) In the same corner there now is a **face with hand raised** as if to bless the chapel.

Some of the key stones appear to have been tampered with over the years – the original guides of 1798 only mention a hand being raised, and despite their meticulous descriptions do not mention a face alongside it. Nowadays people often see the carving as a sign of God Blessing the Work, but this simplistic viewpoint does not ring true with the overall design of Rosslyn. Likewise there was a **simple crescent moon** in the opposite edge of this section of roof carvings and it has been tampered with so much the original moon shape is hard to discern. **The Sun and a dove** can also be spotted among the stars, with the **four archangels** opposite,

Michael hovering above William Sinclair on his capital below. Both Michael and William hold the swords of truth – their proximity to one another hint at the mission that William was leading in building Rosslyn, for he was attempting to map out our journey home, that is under the guidance and protection of the archangel Michael.

During the first stage of Rosslyn's current process of preservation, an unexpected and very local supply of sandstone was discovered, which was used to repair the foundations of the lower chapel /crypt. It is very likely that these stones have now returned to their original construction site, for they could well have formed part of the original castle that stood on College Hill. When Rosslyn was built there would have been a ready surplus of stones to rebuild with. The story of the chapel seems to have come full circle in many ways, and now it is up to us to carry the story forward onto new levels of awareness!

Appendices

Appendix A: Tours

We offer tours of at least four days duration for individuals and small groups to Rosslyn and also other places connected energetically to Rosslyn and Knights Templar in Scotland. These tours are flexible and can include legends, general historical information and esoteric information unless client specify otherwise. Dowsing can be taught in addition at the appropriate sites.

Also we offer workshops/tours of the Burren in County Clare/Galway in Ireland to connect with the Earth in a deeper way using sound, dowsing and Gaia Touch exercises at hidden sites.

www.earthwise.me

www.celtictrails.co.uk

FB: earthwiseconnect

Enquiries jackiequeally@gmail.com

Appendix B: Contact Details

1. Reverend Maia Nartoomid has been an akashic channel for thirty nine years. Her Spirit Mythos website is extensive, containing much of her written work and Spirit Art. PDF files of her earlier writings are also available:

http://www.spiritmythos.org

2. William Buehler

roslinne@fairpoint.net

3. Barry Dunford, author of "The Holy Land of Scotland: Jesus in Scotland and the Gospel of the Grail". An historical researcher, specializing in the early Celtic history of Scotland and the greater British Isles, and local tour guide to the sacred sites of Highland Perthshire, Scotland. www.sacredconnections.co.uk

Appendix C: Names of ENNEAD ANGELS according to Maia/Thoth

1) Al'hoa'ateme

2) Nirsumanasa

3) Ei'irunikohn'na

4) Hav'enapa

5) Sanusemi

6) Ziu'nukatami

7) Tapeket'nake

8) Nuluoinale'atemu

9) Raseme'shinai

Appendix D: Two Studies in Astronomy

Study One: Thoughts on Rosslyn by Jeff Nisbet

There is an ongoing confusion in the sources about Dedication Date vs. Consecration Date. I don't think they are the same thing. There is also an ongoing confusion about the difference between the layoin out a Foundation Stone and the laying of a Cornerstone. I don't think that they are the same, although different researchers seem to use them interchangeably (I think I may be aparty, too). A Foundation Stone would, I think, be the first stone laid in the foundation of a building and a Cornerstone would be the first stone laid on top of the foundation (therefore the only stone of the two to remain visible above the ground).

Rosslyn Chapel was founded upon St. Matthew's Day, 21st September, 1446, and officially dedicated to that saint on the same day in 1450. Since September 21 marks the Autumnal Equinox, when the sun rises exactly due east of Rosslyn, I decided to see if the Earl had written something in the sky above, that might have reflected the truth he'd been carving on the earth below. I wasn't disappointed.

When Rosslyn was dedicated on September 21, 1450, the sun had risen exactly due east. Throughout the day, behind the sun and in exact alignment with the Earth lay the planets Saturn and Neptune, a conjunction that occurs only once every 36 years. And they all rose invisibly in the light of day within the constellation Virgo, symbolic of various Goddesses found in diverse astrological traditions.

To Earth's east, if we include the Sun and Moon, six denizens of our solar system lay within just 30 degrees of sky—all but one of those lying within seven degrees—a surprisingly rare tight grouping.

If you look at the Starchart of Sept. 21, 1450, Rosslyn's dedication date, you'll find that the Sun, Neptune, Saturn and also the Earth are in an alignment of three planets (one undiscovered at the time) and a star (our Sun). The star Zaniah, in Virgo, is also part of that exact alignment, which makes three planets and two stars, equaling five aligned heavenly bodies. The star Porrima, also in Virgo, is very close the alignment, which makes six. And the planet Venus is soon to follow, which makes SEVEN. Actually, now that I think of it, the planet Mercury rose just shortly before any of them, so an argument could be made that there were EIGHT heavenly bodies a narrow area of sky, although only five of them would have been planets (the three others being stars). The resonant significance of the constellation Virgo and its two stars, Zaniah and Porrima, are explained in his article, **Secrets of Rosslyn Chapel.**

Jeff Nisbet's details of how an inverted Cross of Lorraine is encoded in the ceiling at Rosslyn makes a fascinating red at **Rosslyn Chapel Revisited**

http://www.mythomorph.com/

Jeff enjoys investigating and discovering "subtexts" that he believes are written between and beneath the lines of both"history" and "myth"–subtexts that ring closer to actual truth thanthe subject matter he was taught in USA grade school.

Study Two:
Skycharts Equinoctial Celestial Alignments at Rosslyn

By Rab Wilkie

Skycharts for sunrise at the autumn equinox (St Matthew's Day) As seen from Rosslyn in AD 1446 and 2008.

Roslin: 55N52, 3W12
Equinox 2008: 22Sep GMT; sunrise: 5:59am GMT
Equinox 1446: 14Sep GMT; sunrise: 5:58am GMT
Direction: due East (90.0 azimuth)
Borthwick church: 111 degrees, (21 degrees south of East).

Celestial alignments of sacred sites and churches are not uncommon, especially among older churches which were by custom aligned to the rising sun on the calendar date of the day of the saint to which a church was dedicated, so there is nothing extraordinary about Rosslyn Chapel being oriented due east in the direction of sunrise at the Equinoxes because the Day of St Matthew–the saint to which the Chapel was dedicated–was established by the Roman Church to coincide with the Spring Equinox. And since east-west alignments may be the most common anyway, irrespective of a church's dedication, Rosslyn's alignment may be thought of as perfectly prosaic. However, there are additional phenomena that make Rosslyn's situation unique.

At the March equinox three constellations rise with the Sun: Virgo, Leo, and Crater. They are anciently associated with a divine Maiden or Goddess, the Lion/King, and a sacred Cup or Grail. Over time, the constellations associated with the equinox change, but for the last five hundred years or so they have shifted only a bit. Now, as in 1446 when the Chapel was built, the same three constellations rise with the Sun on Saint Matthews's Day.

These three adjacent constellations fill a triangular region of the sky with Leo uppermost and Crater south from Virgo—the constellation through which the Sun is passing on September 21st. But the Lion, which heralds the Sun's rise, can be 'couchant' or 'rampant' depending on latitude. Northward from Edinburgh, the Lion begins to lie down, and Close to the equator he's almost falling over backwards, but within the latitudinal zone around 55 north his head is upright as he stands, much like it is on the Lion Rampant Flag of Scotland.

At Rosslyn's latitude the Grail rises at the same moment as the Sun, but as we head further north the Grail rises later and southward sooner. In 1446 the coordinated rise of Sun and Grail was much more precise.

Furthermore, the brightest star of Crater rises 21 degrees south of east, in line with Borthwick church, the Borthwicks having been cup-bearers to the Sinclairs.

Also in 1446, the Sun rose in conjunction with the star Porrima, named by the Romans after their ancient goddess of prophecy. The link here could be with the gospel of Matthew insofar as it's the astrological gospel—with the Christmas story and the coming of the Magi (astrologers) who saw "His star in the east".

The Sun now rises in Virgo, although no longer with Porrima. Instead, it now rises with Zavijava, made famous at the September equinox in 1922 when it was used to test Einstein's 'prophecy' about the speed of light. (He was right).

In 1446 on Saint Matthew's Day, Jupiter aligned with Denebola in Leo, the 'stand-in' star for our invisible or transcendent Sun, Mazuriel, on a higher plane of reality. Jupiter passes Denebola every twelve years, and often thrice within nine months, but even so, an equinoctial alignment is rare; and Jupiter is the planet of expansive, beneficent power and nobility – in this case amplified by the 'Sun behind the Sun', the spiritual source of true royalty.

Other phenomena which may provide clues to the current significance of Rosslyn: currently (1968-2044), sunrise at the September Equinox aligns with constellation Crater (Cup/Grail), located just below and on the back of the Water Snake (Hydra). Narrowing the timeframe to 2000-12, the Sun aligns with the bottom or pit of the Grail.

Also, Orion is due South, Betelgeuse and the figure's upraised hand exactly at 180 degrees azimuth. This is not surprising because that's the stellar geometry now. Orion and Auriga lie opposite the Galactic Centre. The stars of Orion's drawn Sword/Club and the four 'horses' of Auriga align precisely during 2000-2012 with the June Solstice.

Due North, and quite far above the horizon, is the red eye of the (Pen)Dragon, Eltanin. (The Pendragon's throat passes the zenith at the latitude of Roslin).

Due West, Uranus in Aquarius has just set, as it zigzags during the year back & forth across the cusp with Pisces, (the Aquarian Age cusp).

The Grail constellation is right below the Borthwick azimuth (111), and when the Sun, having risen, aligns with 111 at after 7am, the whole Grail has just appeared above the horizon further south.

Line of sight from Rosslyn relative to the altitude of the visual horizon might reveal other alignments. Irrespective of time of year, Orion (Rigel & Saiph in particular), now rises in the 111 direction. When Rigel passes this azimuth, it is four degrees (420 degrees) above the ideal horizon, and could be right on the real horizon... depending on landscape & hills.

In summary, the Chapel's alignments, East & 111, appear to take both stars and planets into consideration, enabling the link between mundane astrology and transcendent or 'ascendant' light work—quite literally since sunrise on the September equinox includes Leo and the whole complex of Sun, Denebola/Mazuriel, and the Grail (plus 1446 Jupiter). In astrological terms, they are all 'on the Ascendant'.

The Grail Constellation lies just below the horizon at the 111 zone. At the latitude of Rosslyn, Denebola/Mazuriel currently passes due East after ideal sunrise and possibly at the time of equinoctial sunrise as seen on the horizon from Rosslyn. The 'Lyon' (Leo) has just risen–its tail, Denebola, having just cleared the horizon–as the Crater (Grail) clears the ideal horizon.

Leo and its brightest star, Regulus, are associated with royalty and the Lion flag of Scotland. In 2011-12 Regulus is the last bright zodiacal star to shift precessionally into its next zodiacal sign, in this case Virgo. Just a few centuries after the advent of the Piscean Age (70BC–AD70), such stars began moving out of their signs, and it will have taken almost 2000 years to complete the process.

From 2012, all constellations will have shifted one sign, in effect setting the stage for the union of The Lion & The Virgin and also The Scorpion & The Archer, The Grail Bearer and The Fish, and so on around the zodiac, uniting stellar/galactic and solar/terrestrial realms.

Rab Wilkie is a Perth-born anthropologist and astrologer now resident in Peterborough, Ontario.

Email: **rab@peterboro.net**

Website: **www.astrocyclics.com**

This guide written by Jackie Queally (Celtic Trails) is based on several years experience guiding visitors around Rosslyn Chapel long before popular interest in Rosslyn intensified. In the guide Jackie extends her unique basic tour by giving more explicit information on several aspects, including the Reshel which is a body of sacred knowledge that was known to the ancients and utilized here by an inner core of Knights Templar. The Reshel is a dynamic system and still active today. Her hope is that this guide will deepen your perspective on Rosslyn and its spiritual role. The exquisite hand drawings are by Andrew Gilmour a retired architect and academic who has greatly enhanced the guide through his kind efforts.

The Reshel is based on the ancient Hebrew letters generally called "proto-Sinaitic glyphs". These appear to be encoded in the chapel carvings. In this light the stones can be seen as manifestations of deep spiritual mysteries.

www.ingramcontent.com/pod-product-compliance
Lightning Source LLC
Chambersburg PA
CBHW020806160426
43192CB00006B/463